AMAZING ORIGAMI
DINOSAURS
PAPER DINOSAURS ARE FUN TO FOLD!

10 DINOSAUR DESIGNS

32 TEAR-OUT SHEETS

SHUFUNOTOMO

TUTTLE Publishing

Tokyo | Rutland, Vermont | Singapore

T000136I

CONTENTS

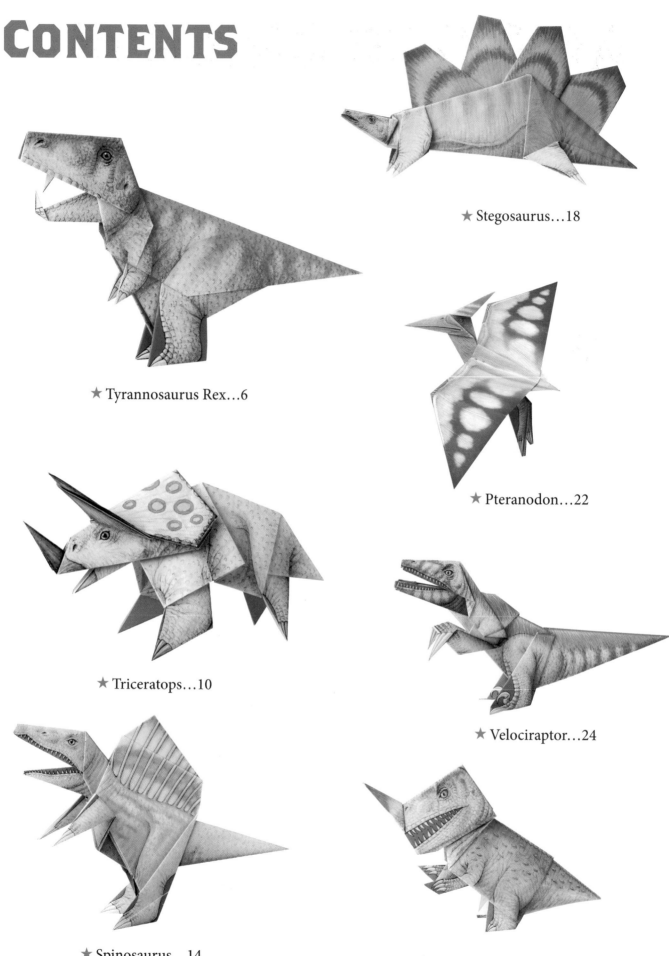

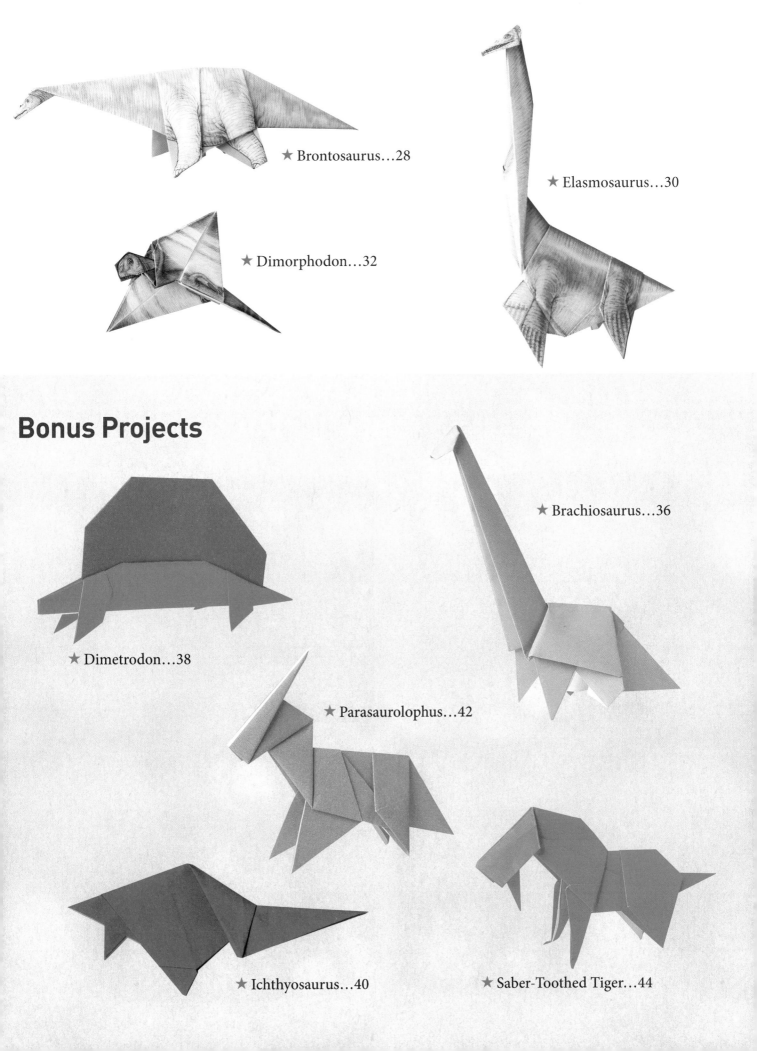

Bonus Projects

Basic Folds

Valley Fold
Fold so the line is on the inside.
In this book, red lines represent valley folds.

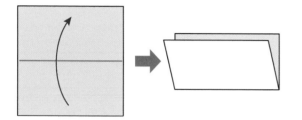

Mountain Fold
Fold so the line is on the outside.
In this book, blue lines represent mountain folds.

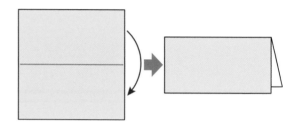

Inside Reverse Fold
Make a mountain fold on each side of the folded paper and then push in the center.

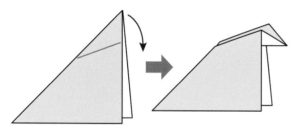

Outside Reverse Fold
Make a valley fold on each side of the folded paper and then invert the corner.

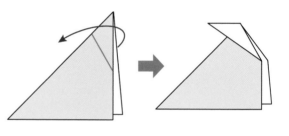

Crimp Fold
This fold combines an inside reverse fold and an outside reverse fold.
There are various ways to make this fold.

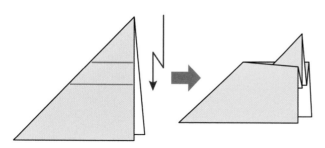

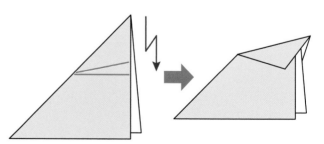

Base Folds A & B

These basic forms are used to make the Tyrannosaurus Rex, Velociraptor, Parasaurolophus, Ceratosaurus, Brontosaurus, Brachiosaurus, Ichthyosaurus, Elasmosaurus, and the Saber-toothed Tiger. Practice making these bases so that you can fold them quickly and easily. Lift up the back part of Base A to make Base B.

1

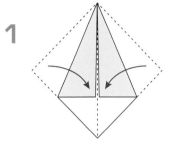

With the origami paper reverse-side up and one corner at the top, fold the left and right corners into the center. Turn the paper over.

2

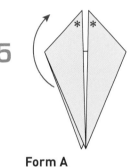

Fold the paper in half, making a valley fold along line A.

3

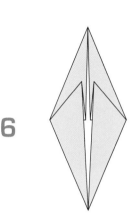

Turn the paper over again.

4

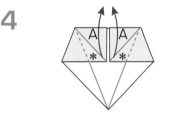

Lift up the parts marked A and fold the opened sections up into the center.

5

Form A
The completed Base A.

6

Form B
This form is completed when you lift up the back part of Base A.

Base Fold C — Crane Base

This is the same basic folded form used to make an origami crane, and it's used in this book to make the Triceratops, Spinosaurus, Pteranodon, Velociraptor, and Dimorphodon.

1

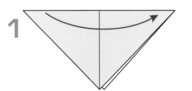

Fold the paper into a triangle and then fold it in half.

2

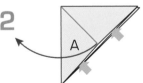

Fold the part marked A outward to the left to create a square.

3

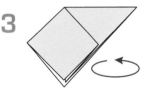

Turn the paper over horizontally.

4

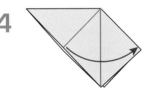

Fold the other side outward in the same way as in step 2.

5

Fold parts marked A into the center and then open them out again to make crease lines.

6

Slightly lift up corner B and fold the parts labeled A inward (inside reverse folds).

7

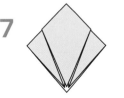

Turn the paper over and repeat steps 5–6.

8

The completed Base C (Crane Base).

Tyrannosaurus Rex

This well-known dinosaur was one of the strongest and largest carnivorous animals to have ever walked the Earth. It lived in the Late Cretaceous period (100–65 million years ago) on what is now the North American continent. It preyed upon large herbivorous dinosaurs using its huge mouth lined with sharp teeth. It had remarkably small arms.

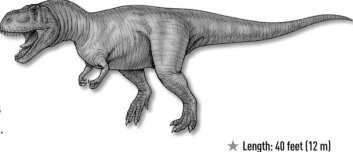

★ Length: 40 feet (12 m)
★ Weight: 7 tons
★ Period: Late Cretaceous

Use the dinosaur pattern origami paper starting on page 47!

—— Valley Fold
—— Mountain Fold

Legs & Lower Jaw

1

Fold Base B (see page 5), and then make a valley fold along the ① lines. Next, pull out parts marked A from the center to the sides.

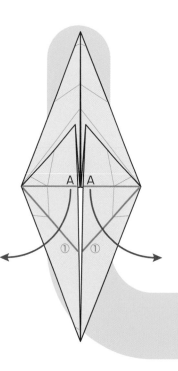

2

Make a mountain fold along line ① to fold it in half vertically.

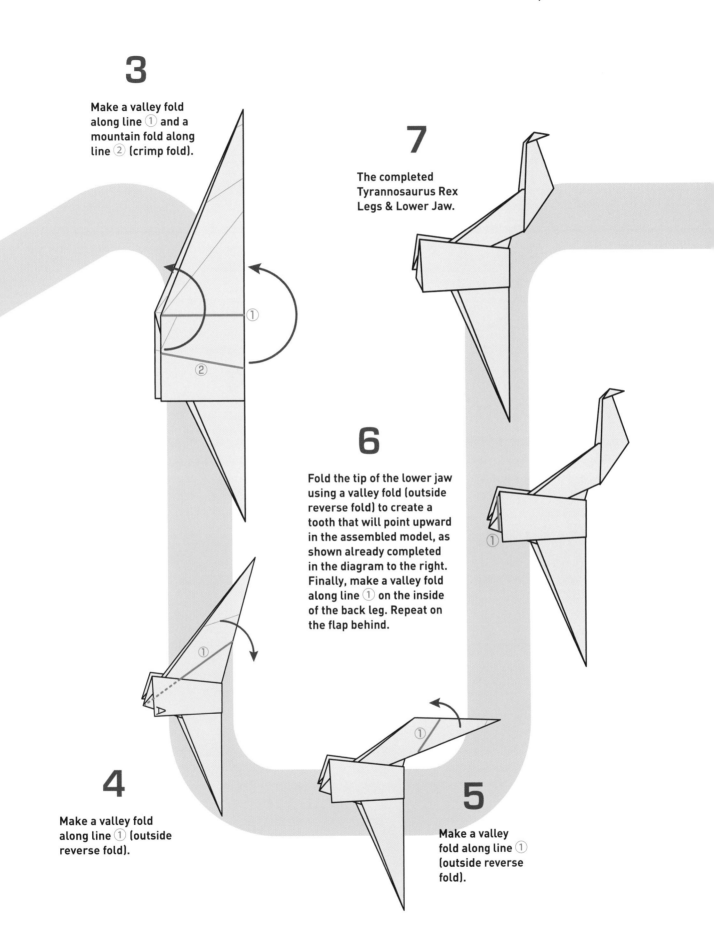

3

Make a valley fold along line ① and a mountain fold along line ② (crimp fold).

7

The completed Tyrannosaurus Rex Legs & Lower Jaw.

6

Fold the tip of the lower jaw using a valley fold (outside reverse fold) to create a tooth that will point upward in the assembled model, as shown already completed in the diagram to the right. Finally, make a valley fold along line ① on the inside of the back leg. Repeat on the flap behind.

4

Make a valley fold along line ① (outside reverse fold).

5

Make a valley fold along line ① (outside reverse fold).

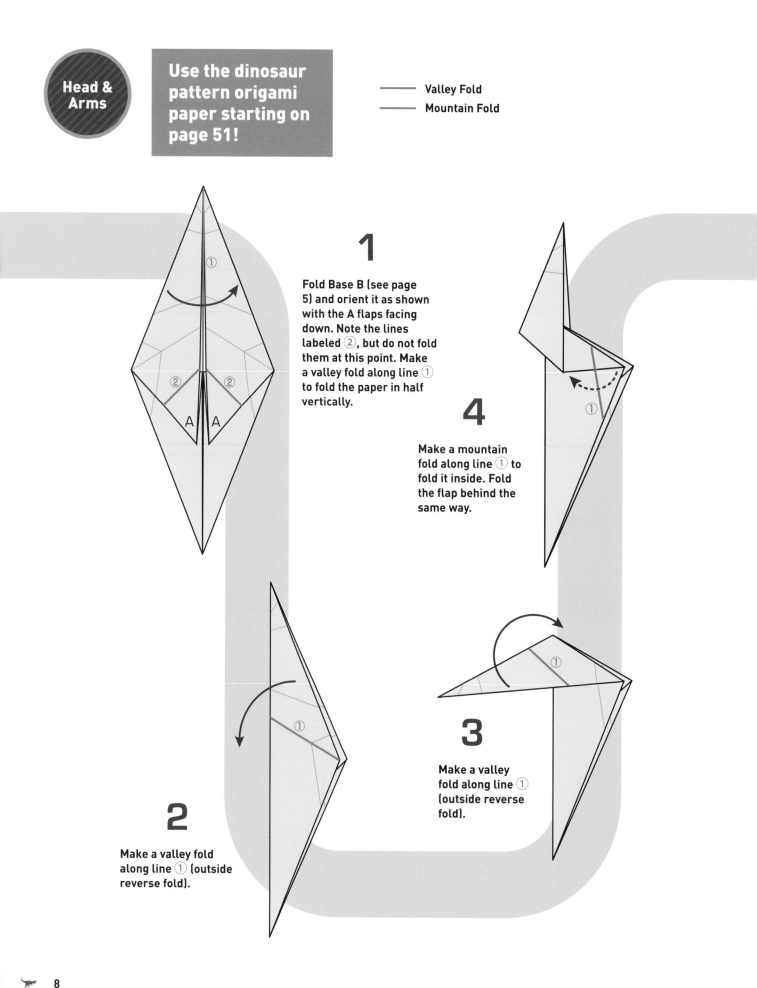

Use the dinosaur pattern origami paper starting on page 51!

—— Valley Fold

—— Mountain Fold

1

Fold Base B (see page 5) and orient it as shown with the A flaps facing down. Note the lines labeled ②, but do not fold them at this point. Make a valley fold along line ① to fold the paper in half vertically.

4

Make a mountain fold along line ① to fold it inside. Fold the flap behind the same way.

3

Make a valley fold along line ① (outside reverse fold).

2

Make a valley fold along line ① (outside reverse fold).

8

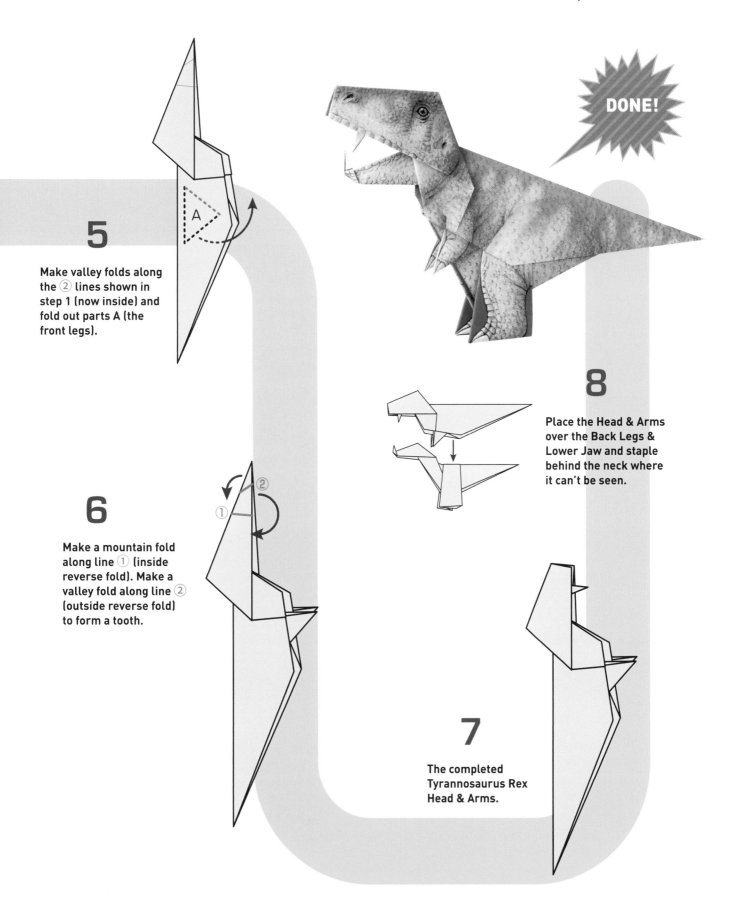

DONE!

5

Make valley folds along the ② lines shown in step 1 (now inside) and fold out parts A (the front legs).

A

6

Make a mountain fold along line ① (inside reverse fold). Make a valley fold along line ② (outside reverse fold) to form a tooth.

① ②

8

Place the Head & Arms over the Back Legs & Lower Jaw and staple behind the neck where it can't be seen.

7

The completed Tyrannosaurus Rex Head & Arms.

Triceratops

This large herbivorous dinosaur lived in the Late Cretaceous period (100–65 million years ago) on what is now the North American continent. It had 3 large horns and a large frilled collar. The horns above its eyes were five feet (1.5 m) long. It had a docile nature and ate leaves and grass.

★ Length: 30 feet (9 m)
★ Weight: 10 tons
★ Period: Late Cretaceous

Use the dinosaur pattern origami paper starting on page 55!

Body

1

Note the line labeled ③, but do not fold it at this point. Cut along the ① lines, make mountain folds along the ② lines, and then turn the paper over. Open out the cut sections.

2

Make mountain folds along the ① lines and valley folds along the ② lines. Then make a mountain fold along line ③ (shown in step 1— now on the back) and fold out part labeled A down to either side.

3

Make valley folds along the ① lines and fold upward.

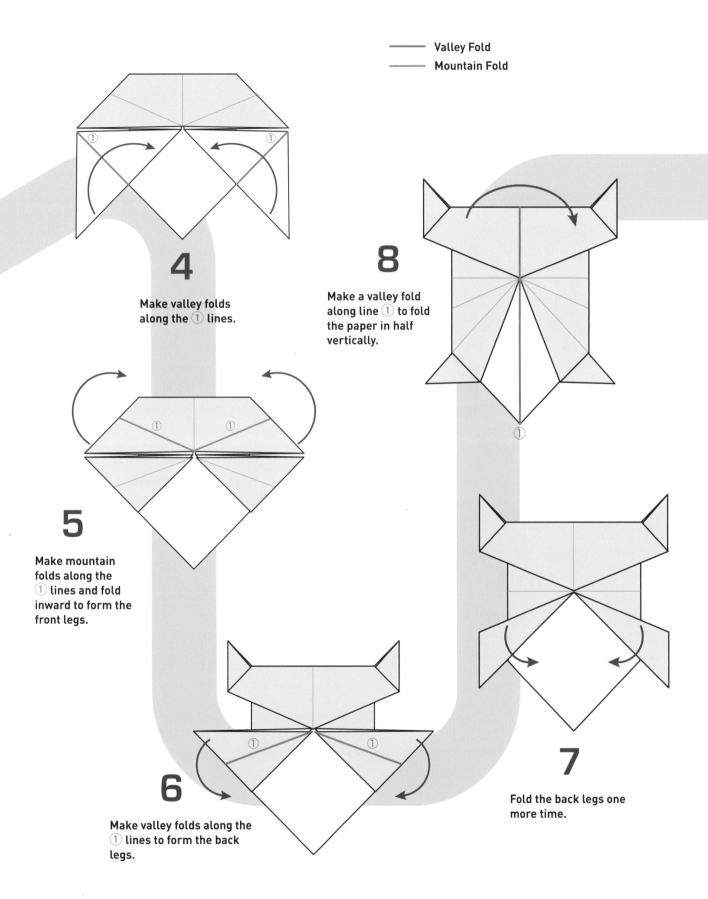

Valley Fold
Mountain Fold

4

Make valley folds along the ① lines.

5

Make mountain folds along the ① lines and fold inward to form the front legs.

6

Make valley folds along the ① lines to form the back legs.

7

Fold the back legs one more time.

8

Make a valley fold along line ① to fold the paper in half vertically.

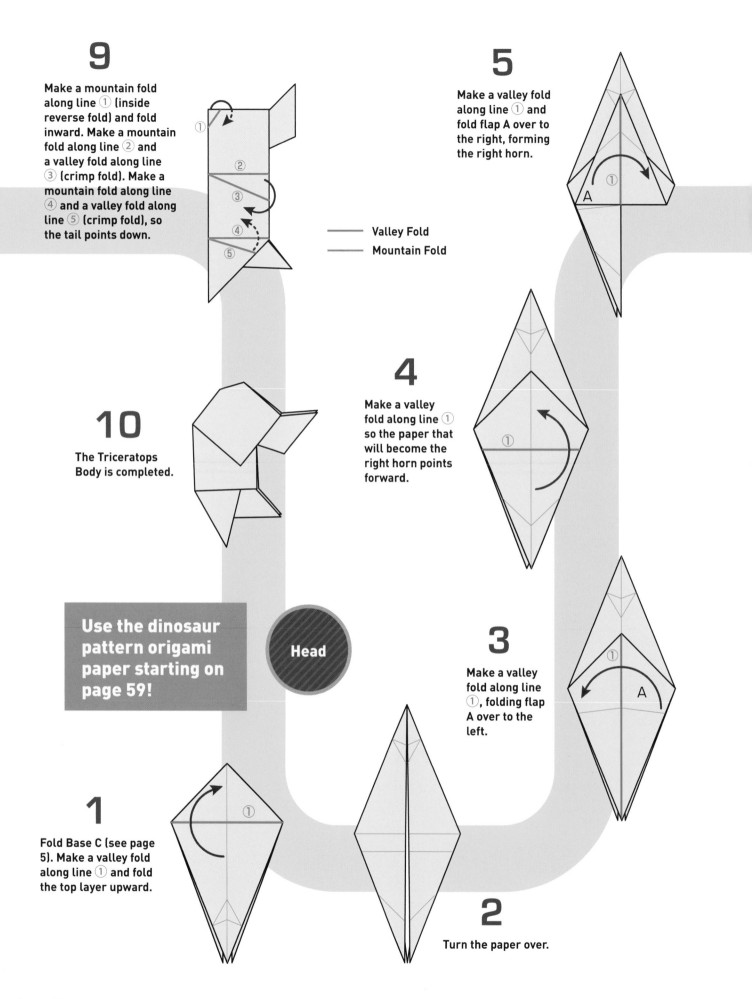

9

Make a mountain fold along line ① (inside reverse fold) and fold inward. Make a mountain fold along line ② and a valley fold along line ③ (crimp fold). Make a mountain fold along line ④ and a valley fold along line ⑤ (crimp fold), so the tail points down.

Valley Fold
Mountain Fold

5

Make a valley fold along line ① and fold flap A over to the right, forming the right horn.

4

Make a valley fold along line ① so the paper that will become the right horn points forward.

10

The Triceratops Body is completed.

Use the dinosaur pattern origami paper starting on page 59!

Head

3

Make a valley fold along line ①, folding flap A over to the left.

1

Fold Base C (see page 5). Make a valley fold along line ① and fold the top layer upward.

2

Turn the paper over.

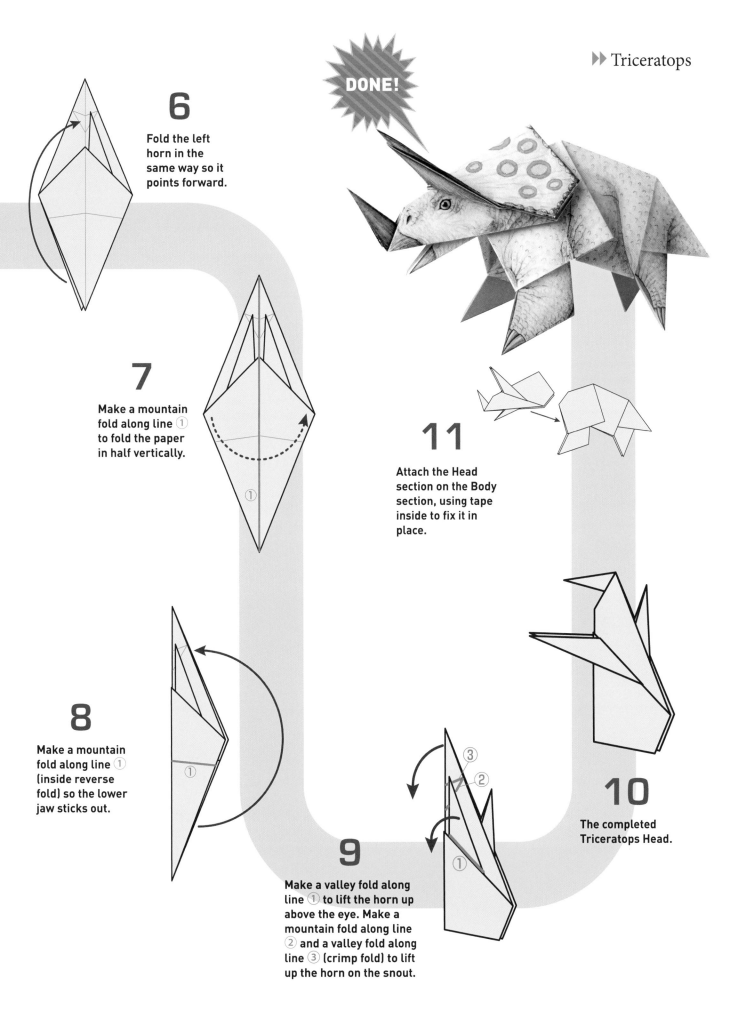

DONE!

6

Fold the left horn in the same way so it points forward.

7

Make a mountain fold along line ① to fold the paper in half vertically.

①

8

Make a mountain fold along line ① (inside reverse fold) so the lower jaw sticks out.

①

9

Make a valley fold along line ① to lift the horn up above the eye. Make a mountain fold along line ② and a valley fold along line ③ (crimp fold) to lift up the horn on the snout.

③
②
①

10

The completed Triceratops Head.

11

Attach the Head section on the Body section, using tape inside to fix it in place.

Spinosaurus

This large carnivorous dinosaur lived in the Late Cretaceous period (100–65 million years ago) on what is now the African continent. It had an elongated head and is believed to have mainly preyed upon on fish in the same way that alligators do today. It had a distinctive large sail on its back.

★ Length: 40 feet (12 m)
★ Weight: 6 tons
★ Period: Late Cretaceous

Use the dinosaur pattern origami paper starting on page 63!

—— Valley Fold
—— Mountain Fold

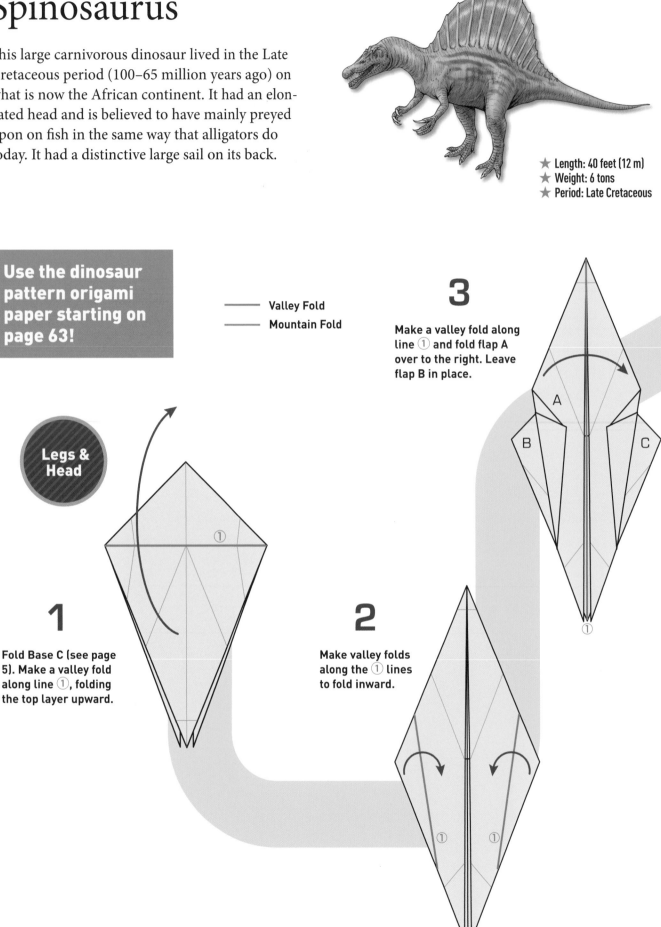

Legs & Head

1

Fold Base C (see page 5). Make a valley fold along line ①, folding the top layer upward.

2

Make valley folds along the ① lines to fold inward.

3

Make a valley fold along line ① and fold flap A over to the right. Leave flap B in place.

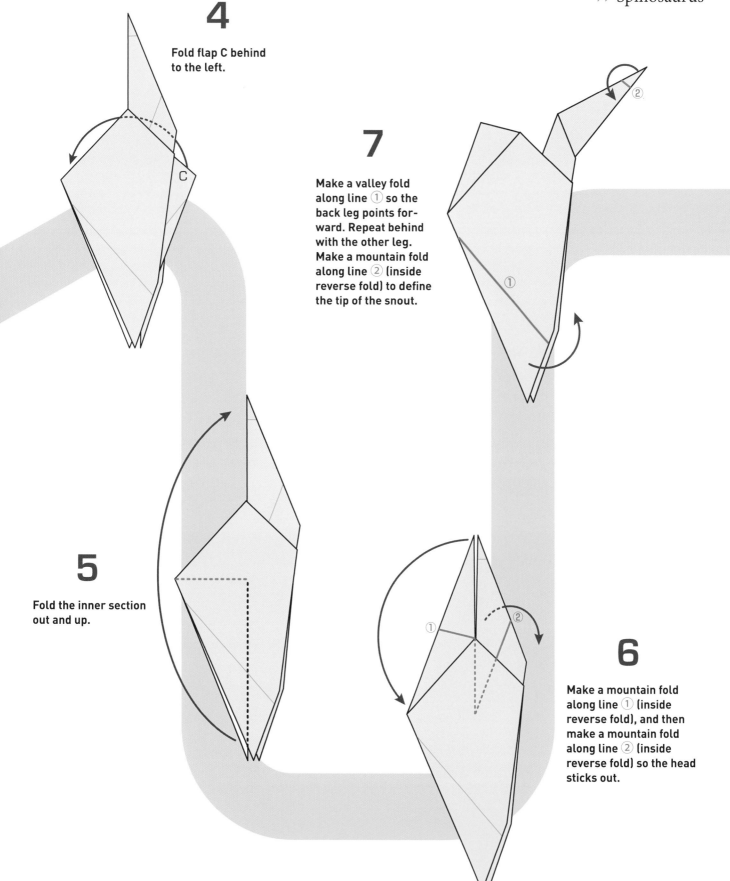

4

Fold flap C behind to the left.

7

Make a valley fold along line ① so the back leg points forward. Repeat behind with the other leg. Make a mountain fold along line ② (inside reverse fold) to define the tip of the snout.

5

Fold the inner section out and up.

6

Make a mountain fold along line ① (inside reverse fold), and then make a mountain fold along line ② (inside reverse fold) so the head sticks out.

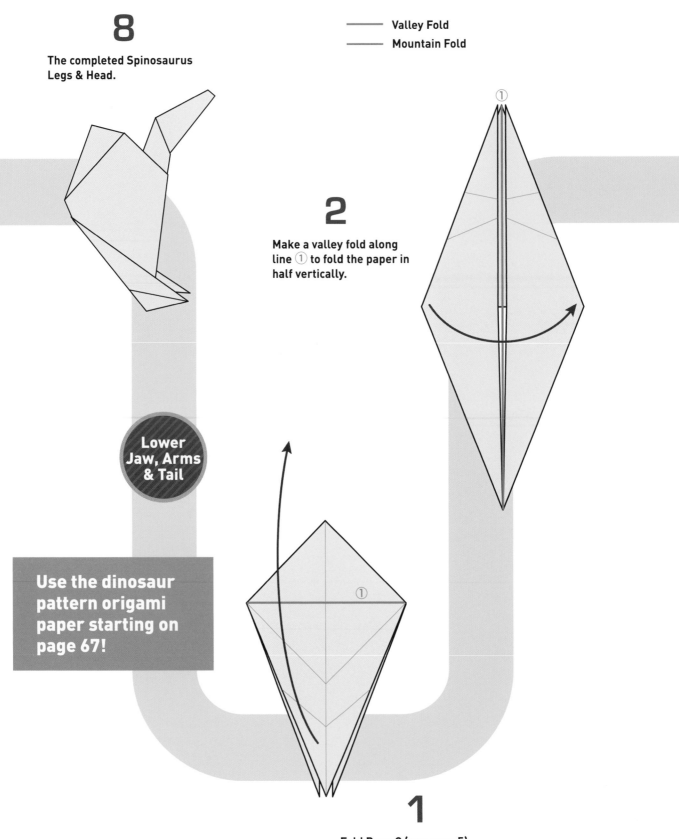

8

The completed Spinosaurus Legs & Head.

Valley Fold
Mountain Fold

2

Make a valley fold along line ① to fold the paper in half vertically.

Lower Jaw, Arms & Tail

Use the dinosaur pattern origami paper starting on page 67!

1

Fold Base C (see page 5). Make a valley fold along line ① and fold both the top layer and center layer upward.

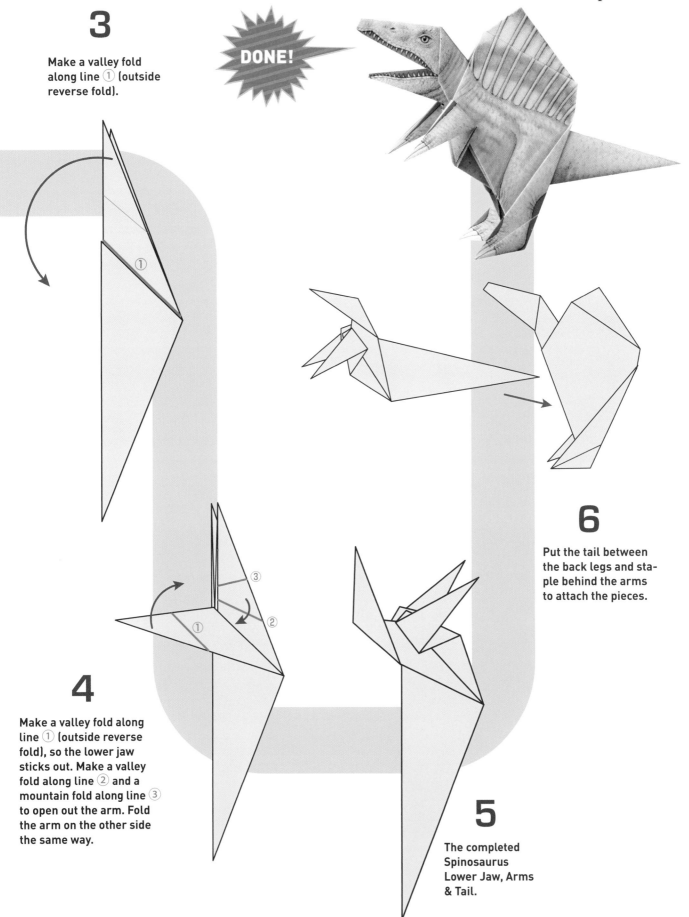

3

Make a valley fold along line ① (outside reverse fold).

DONE!

4

Make a valley fold along line ① (outside reverse fold), so the lower jaw sticks out. Make a valley fold along line ② and a mountain fold along line ③ to open out the arm. Fold the arm on the other side the same way.

6

Put the tail between the back legs and staple behind the arms to attach the pieces.

5

The completed Spinosaurus Lower Jaw, Arms & Tail.

Stegosaurus

This herbivorous dinosaur lived in the Late Jurassic period (170–145 million years ago) on what is now the North American continent. It had fin-like bony plates along its back and a small head compared to its body with a brain only the size of a walnut.

★ Length: 20 feet (6 m)
★ Weight: 2 tons
★ Period: Late Jurassic

Use the dinosaur pattern origami paper starting on page 71!

—— Valley Fold
—— Mountain Fold

Plates

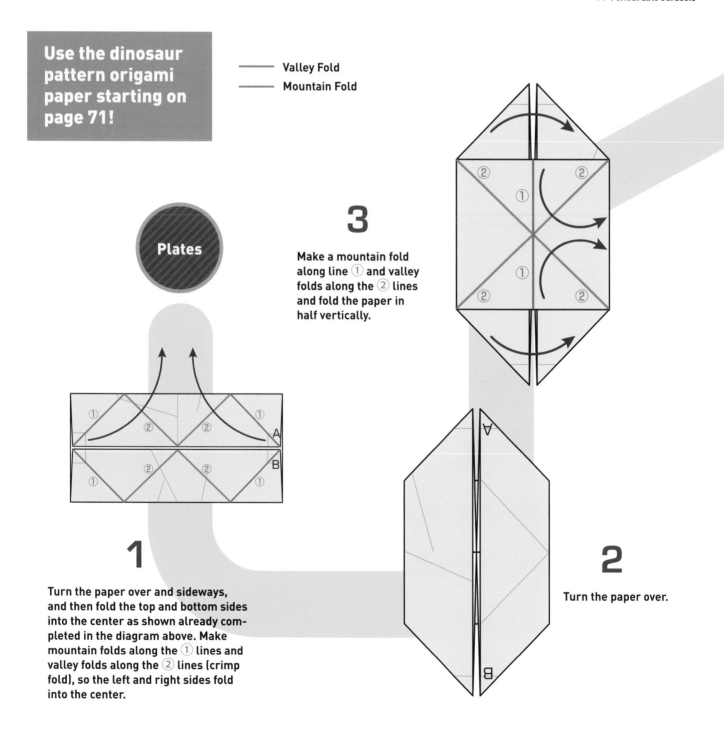

3

Make a mountain fold along line ① and valley folds along the ② lines and fold the paper in half vertically.

1

Turn the paper over and sideways, and then fold the top and bottom sides into the center as shown already completed in the diagram above. Make mountain folds along the ① lines and valley folds along the ② lines (crimp fold), so the left and right sides fold into the center.

2

Turn the paper over.

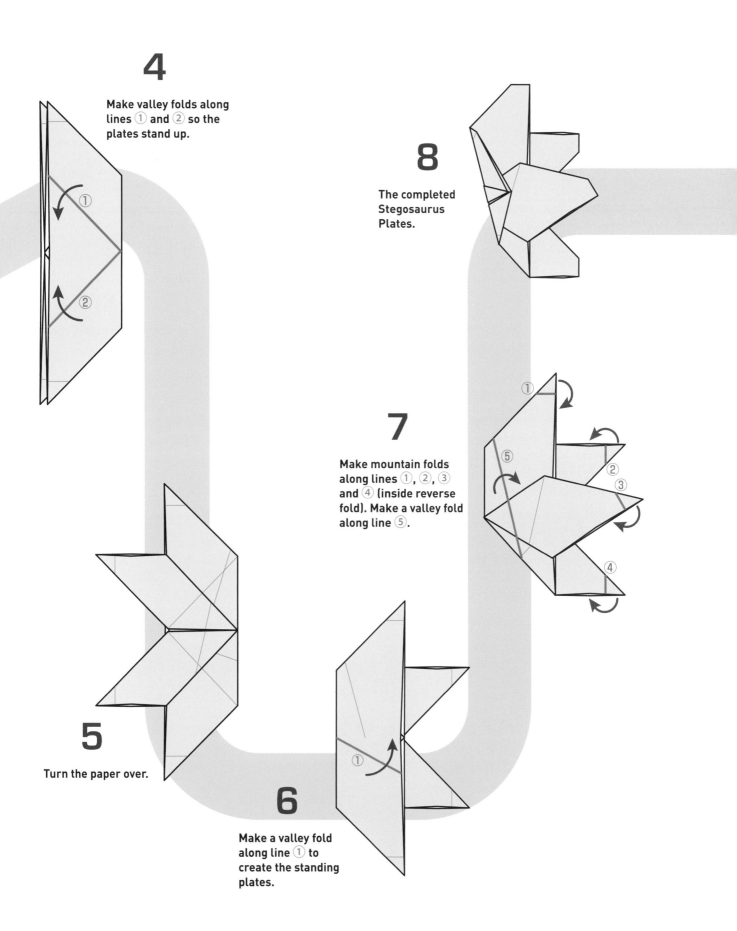

4

Make valley folds along lines ① and ② so the plates stand up.

8

The completed Stegosaurus Plates.

7

Make mountain folds along lines ①, ②, ③ and ④ (inside reverse fold). Make a valley fold along line ⑤.

5

Turn the paper over.

6

Make a valley fold along line ① to create the standing plates.

Use the dinosaur pattern origami paper starting on page 75!

—— Valley Fold
—— Mountain Fold

Body

1

Turn the paper over, and then fold the left and right sides into the center, as shown already completed in the diagram below. Then, make mountain folds along the ① lines (inside reverse fold) and fold inward.

6

Make a valley fold along line ① and a mountain fold along line ②, and then stretch out line ③ so the back legs stick out. Fold the other side the same way.

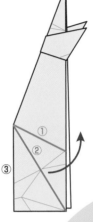

2

Make a valley fold along line ① and fold down the corner marked with the As.

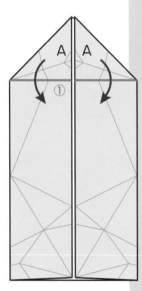

5

Make a mountain fold along line ① to fold it inward. Fold in the other side the same way.

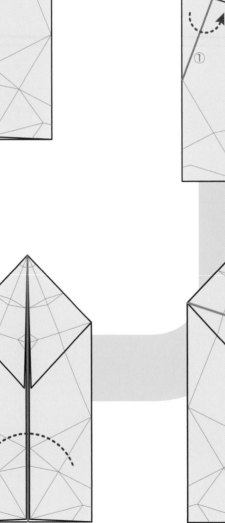

3

Make a mountain fold along line ① to fold the paper in half vertically.

4

Make a valley fold along line ① so the front legs point forward.

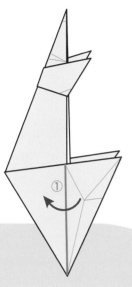

7

Make a valley fold along line ① to lift up the back legs.

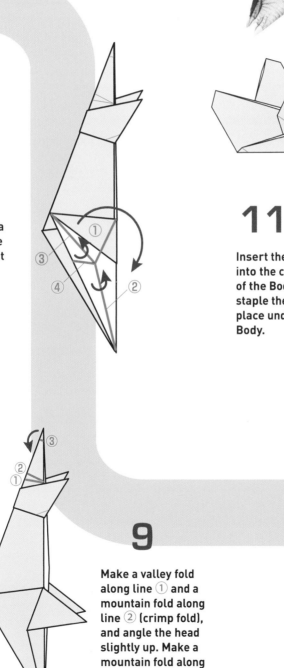

8

Make valley folds along lines ①, ② and ③ and a mountain fold along line ④ so the back legs point downward.

11

Insert the Plates into the center of the Body and staple them into place under the Body.

10

Make a mountain fold along line ① to fold in the bend of the front leg. The Stegosaurus body is completed.

9

Make a valley fold along line ① and a mountain fold along line ② (crimp fold), and angle the head slightly up. Make a mountain fold along line ③ to fold the tip of the snout inside.

Pteranodon

This flying dinosaur, called a Pterosaur, lived in the Late Cretaceous period (99–65 million years ago) on what is now the European and North American continents. Flapping its massive wings required lots of energy, but once aloft it could glide long and far.

★ Wingspan: 23 feet (7 m)
★ Weight: 37½ lbs (17 kg)
★ Period: Late Cretaceous

————— Valley Fold
————— Mountain Fold

Use the dinosaur pattern origami paper starting on page 79!

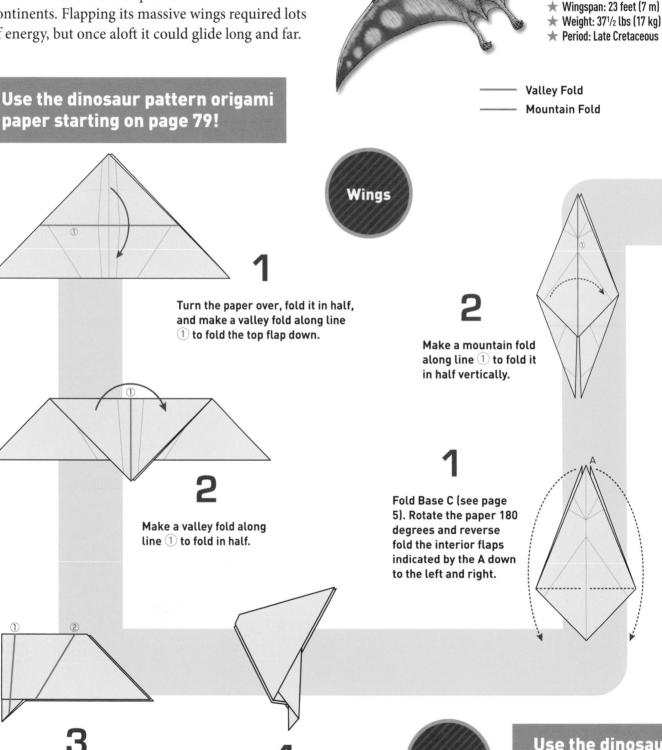

Wings

1

Turn the paper over, fold it in half, and make a valley fold along line ① to fold the top flap down.

2

Make a valley fold along line ① to fold in half.

3

Make a valley fold along line ① and a mountain fold along line ② to fold up the wing. Fold up the other wing the same way.

4

The Pteranodon's completed Wings.

2

Make a mountain fold along line ① to fold it in half vertically.

1

Fold Base C (see page 5). Rotate the paper 180 degrees and reverse fold the interior flaps indicated by the A down to the left and right.

Body

Use the dinosaur pattern origami paper starting on page 83!

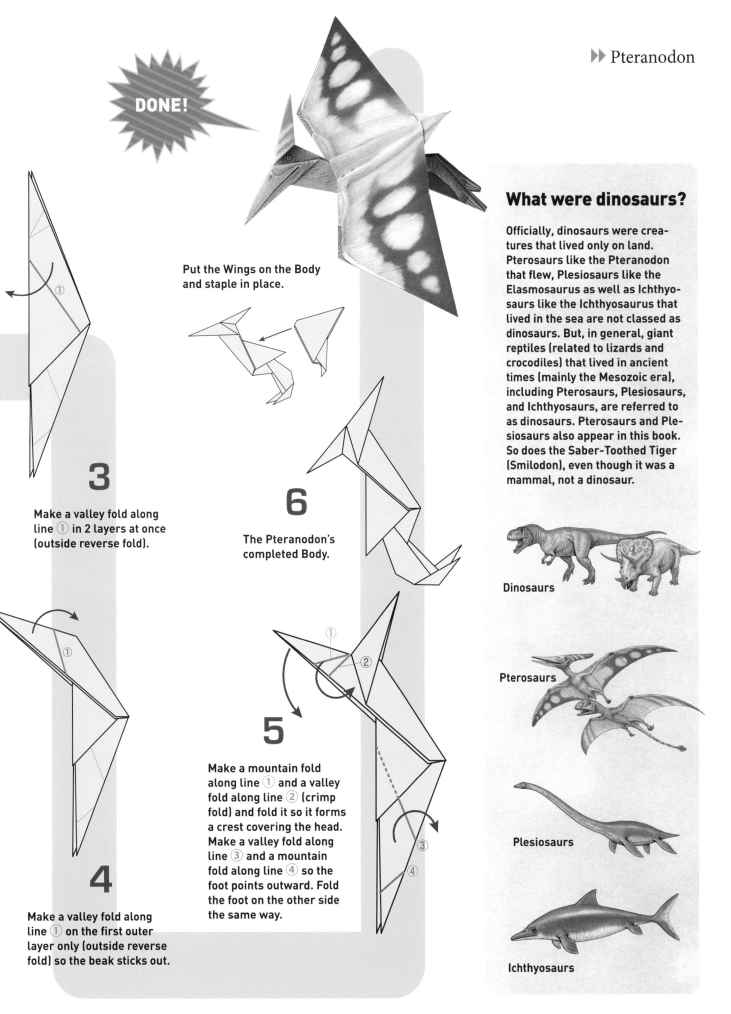

DONE!

Put the Wings on the Body and staple in place.

3

Make a valley fold along line ① in 2 layers at once (outside reverse fold).

6

The Pteranodon's completed Body.

4

Make a valley fold along line ① on the first outer layer only (outside reverse fold) so the beak sticks out.

5

Make a mountain fold along line ① and a valley fold along line ② (crimp fold) and fold it so it forms a crest covering the head. Make a valley fold along line ③ and a mountain fold along line ④ so the foot points outward. Fold the foot on the other side the same way.

What were dinosaurs?

Officially, dinosaurs were creatures that lived only on land. Pterosaurs like the Pteranodon that flew, Plesiosaurs like the Elasmosaurus as well as Ichthyosaurs like the Ichthyosaurus that lived in the sea are not classed as dinosaurs. But, in general, giant reptiles (related to lizards and crocodiles) that lived in ancient times (mainly the Mesozoic era), including Pterosaurs, Plesiosaurs, and Ichthyosaurs, are referred to as dinosaurs. Pterosaurs and Plesiosaurs also appear in this book. So does the Saber-Toothed Tiger (Smilodon), even though it was a mammal, not a dinosaur.

Dinosaurs

Pterosaurs

Plesiosaurs

Ichthyosaurs

Velociraptor

This small carnivorous dinosaur lived in the Late Cretaceous period (99–65 million years ago) on the Asian continent. It had a similar body mass to that of a wolf, and it had feathers on its body. It was a ferocious predator, and tore prey with its sharp teeth and the large claws on its back legs.

★ Height: 6 feet (1.8 m)
★ Weight: 33 lbs (15 kg)
★ Period: Late Cretaceous

Use the dinosaur pattern origami paper starting on page 87!

Head & Front Legs

— Valley Fold
— Mountain Fold

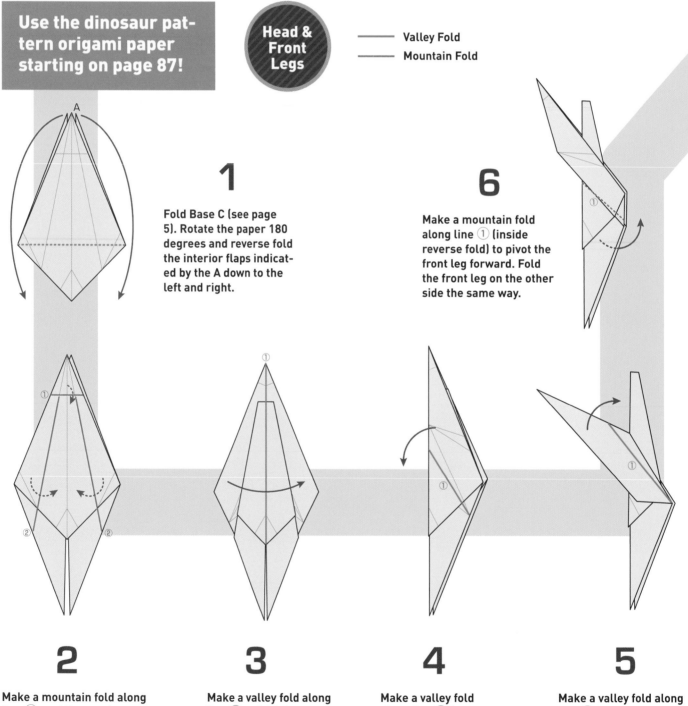

1

Fold Base C (see page 5). Rotate the paper 180 degrees and reverse fold the interior flaps indicated by the A down to the left and right.

6

Make a mountain fold along line ① (inside reverse fold) to pivot the front leg forward. Fold the front leg on the other side the same way.

2

Make a mountain fold along line ①, and then make mountain folds along the ② lines.

3

Make a valley fold along line ① to fold the paper in half vertically.

4

Make a valley fold along line ① (outside reverse fold).

5

Make a valley fold along line ① (outside reverse fold) to form the head.

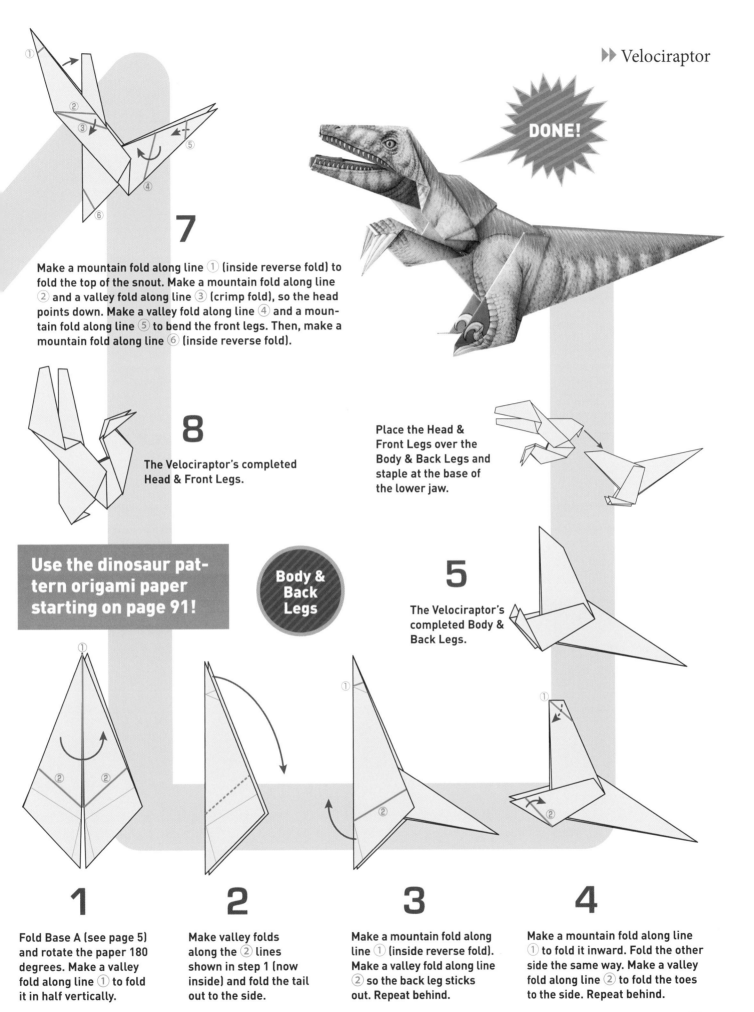

DONE!

7

Make a mountain fold along line ① (inside reverse fold) to fold the top of the snout. Make a mountain fold along line ② and a valley fold along line ③ (crimp fold), so the head points down. Make a valley fold along line ④ and a mountain fold along line ⑤ to bend the front legs. Then, make a mountain fold along line ⑥ (inside reverse fold).

8

The Velociraptor's completed Head & Front Legs.

Place the Head & Front Legs over the Body & Back Legs and staple at the base of the lower jaw.

Use the dinosaur pattern origami paper starting on page 91!

Body & Back Legs

5

The Velociraptor's completed Body & Back Legs.

1

Fold Base A (see page 5) and rotate the paper 180 degrees. Make a valley fold along line ① to fold it in half vertically.

2

Make valley folds along the ② lines shown in step 1 (now inside) and fold the tail out to the side.

3

Make a mountain fold along line ① (inside reverse fold). Make a valley fold along line ② so the back leg sticks out. Repeat behind.

4

Make a mountain fold along line ① to fold it inward. Fold the other side the same way. Make a valley fold along line ② to fold the toes to the side. Repeat behind.

Ceratosaurus

This dinosaur, related to the Tyrannosaurus Rex, lived in the late Jurassic period (170–145 million years ago) on what is now the North American continent. It was on the smaller side, and had a horn on its snout and small horns above its eyes. It had small spikes along its back, too.

★ Length: 20 feet (6 m)
★ Weight: 1,100 lbs (500 kg)
★ Period: Late Jurassic

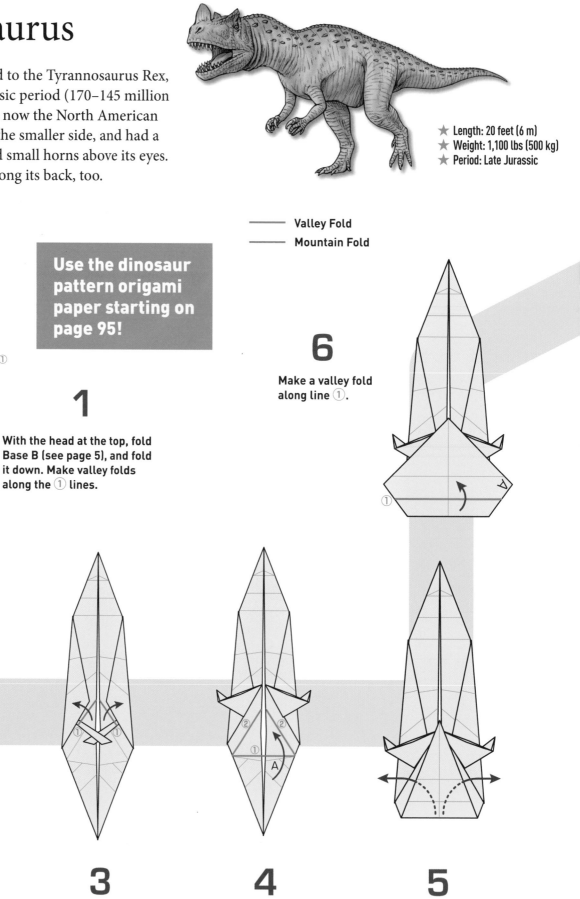

——— Valley Fold
——— Mountain Fold

Use the dinosaur pattern origami paper starting on page 95!

1

With the head at the top, fold Base B (see page 5), and fold it down. Make valley folds along the ① lines.

6

Make a valley fold along line ①.

2

Make valley folds along the ① lines.

3

Make valley folds along the ① lines so the front legs point to the sides.

4

Make a valley fold along line ① to fold the tail upward.

5

Make valley folds along the ② lines shown in step 4 (now inside) and open flap A to the sides.

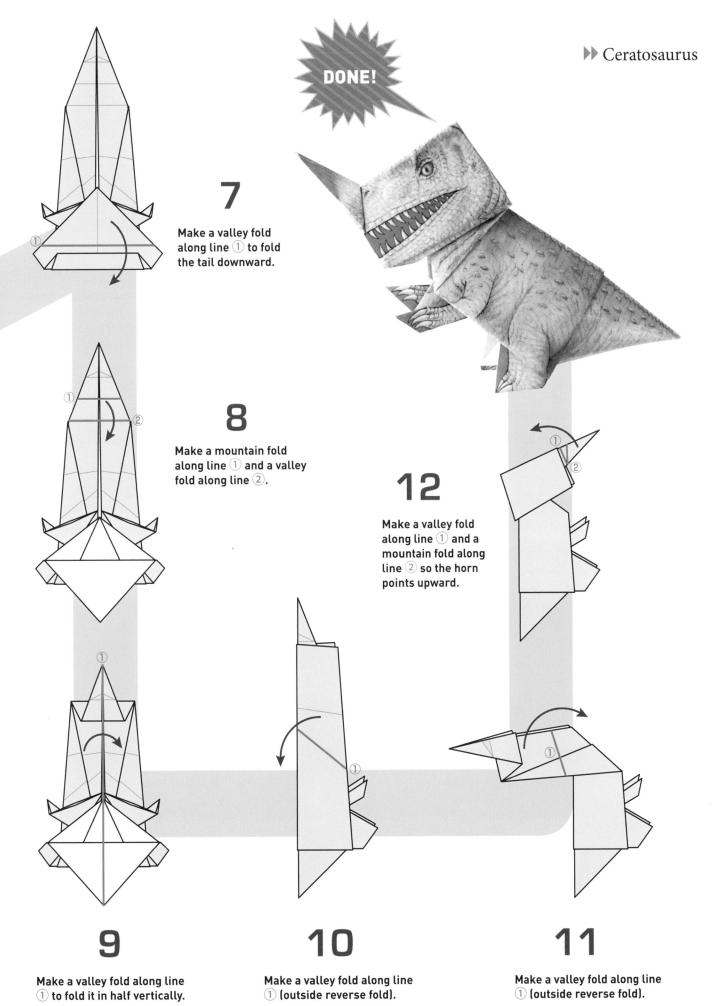

DONE!

7

Make a valley fold along line ① to fold the tail downward.

8

Make a mountain fold along line ① and a valley fold along line ②.

12

Make a valley fold along line ① and a mountain fold along line ② so the horn points upward.

9

Make a valley fold along line ① to fold it in half vertically.

10

Make a valley fold along line ① (outside reverse fold).

11

Make a valley fold along line ① (outside reverse fold).

Brontosaurus

This large herbivorous dinosaur, recently also called Apatosaurus, lived in the late Jurassic period (170–145 million years ago) on what is now the North American continent. It stood on its back legs to eat leaves in tall trees. Many moved around in herds.

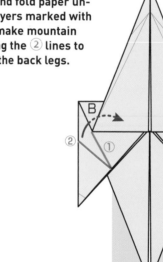

★ Length: 70 feet (21 m)
★ Weight: 30 tons
★ Period: Late Jurassic

Use the dinosaur pattern origami paper starting on page 99!

———— Valley Fold
———— Mountain Fold

3

Make valley folds along the ① lines and fold paper under the layers marked with B. Then, make mountain folds along the ② lines to open out the back legs.

B   B
② ①   ① ②

1

Fold Base A (see page 5) and rotate the paper 180 degrees. Fold down the back part. Make valley folds along lines ① and open parts A to the sides to form the head and tail.

A A

2

Make a valley fold along line ① to fold the head upward.

①

A   A

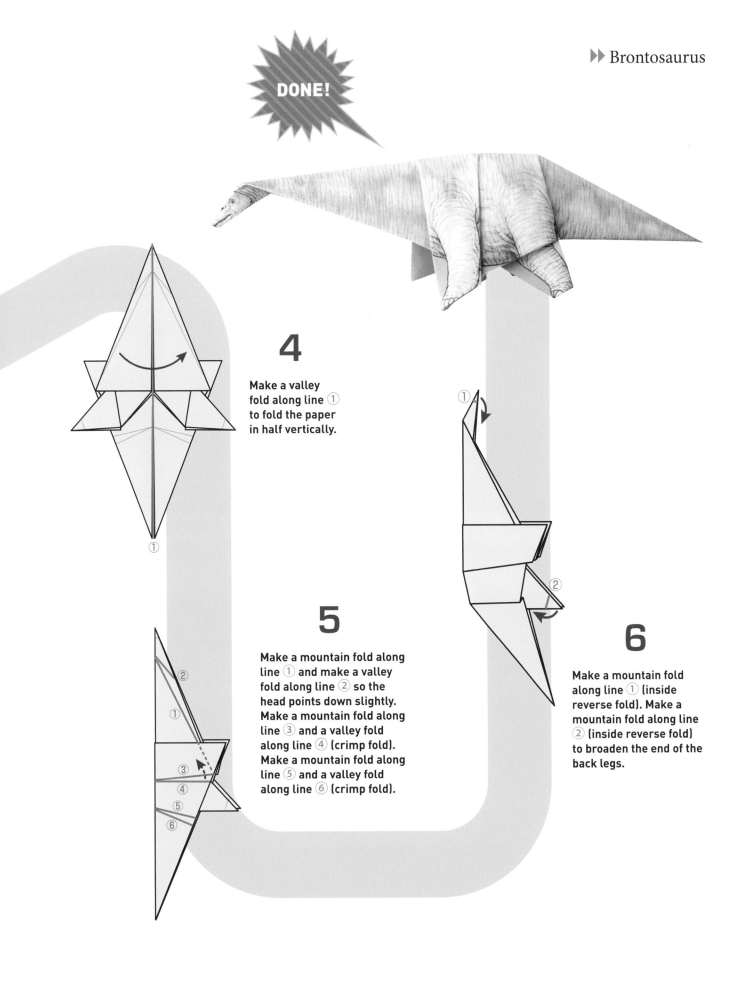

DONE!

4

Make a valley fold along line ① to fold the paper in half vertically.

5

Make a mountain fold along line ① and make a valley fold along line ② so the head points down slightly. Make a mountain fold along line ③ and a valley fold along line ④ (crimp fold). Make a mountain fold along line ⑤ and a valley fold along line ⑥ (crimp fold).

6

Make a mountain fold along line ① (inside reverse fold). Make a mountain fold along line ② (inside reverse fold) to broaden the end of the back legs.

Elasmosaurus

This reptile inhabited the sea in the Late Cretaceous period (99–65 million years ago) and was a type of Plesiosaur. It had a distinctive long neck and paddle-shaped limbs, and it preyed upon fish. Fossils of the Futabasaurus (related to the Elasmosaurus) have been found in Japan.

★ Length: 34 feet (10 m)
★ Weight: 20 tons
★ Period: Late Cretaceous

Use the dinosaur pattern origami paper starting on page 103!

—— Valley Fold
—— Mountain Fold

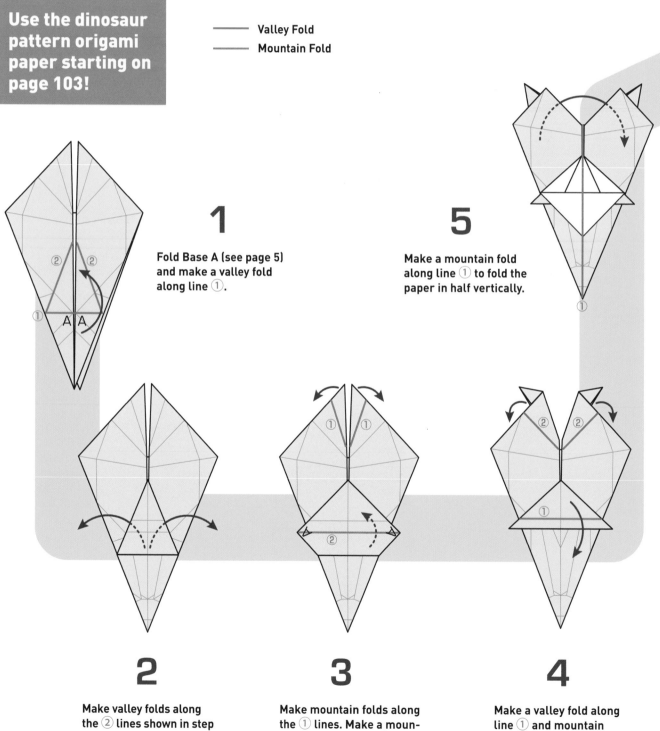

1
Fold Base A (see page 5) and make a valley fold along line ①.

5
Make a mountain fold along line ① to fold the paper in half vertically.

2
Make valley folds along the ② lines shown in step 1 (now inside) and open the A flaps to the sides.

3
Make mountain folds along the ① lines. Make a mountain fold along line ②.

4
Make a valley fold along line ① and mountain folds along the ② lines.

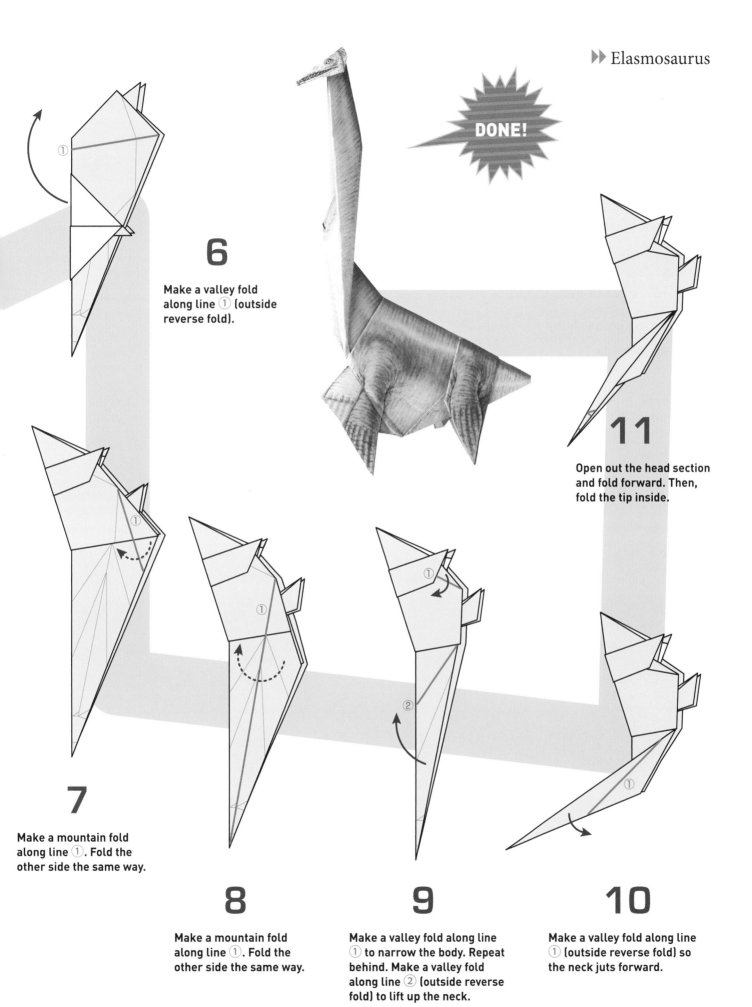

DONE!

6

Make a valley fold along line ① (outside reverse fold).

7

Make a mountain fold along line ①. Fold the other side the same way.

8

Make a mountain fold along line ①. Fold the other side the same way.

9

Make a valley fold along line ① to narrow the body. Repeat behind. Make a valley fold along line ② (outside reverse fold) to lift up the neck.

10

Make a valley fold along line ① (outside reverse fold) so the neck juts forward.

11

Open out the head section and fold forward. Then, fold the tip inside.

Dimorphodon

This early Pterosaur lived in the early Jurassic period (199–170 million years ago) on what is now the European continent. It was relatively small, with a large round head and long tail, and it was thought to have eaten insects and lizards.

★ Wingspan: 4 feet (1.2 m)
★ Weight: 6.6–8.8 (3–5 kg)
★ Period: Late Jurassic

Use the dinosaur pattern origami paper starting on page 107!

—— Valley Fold
—— Mountain Fold

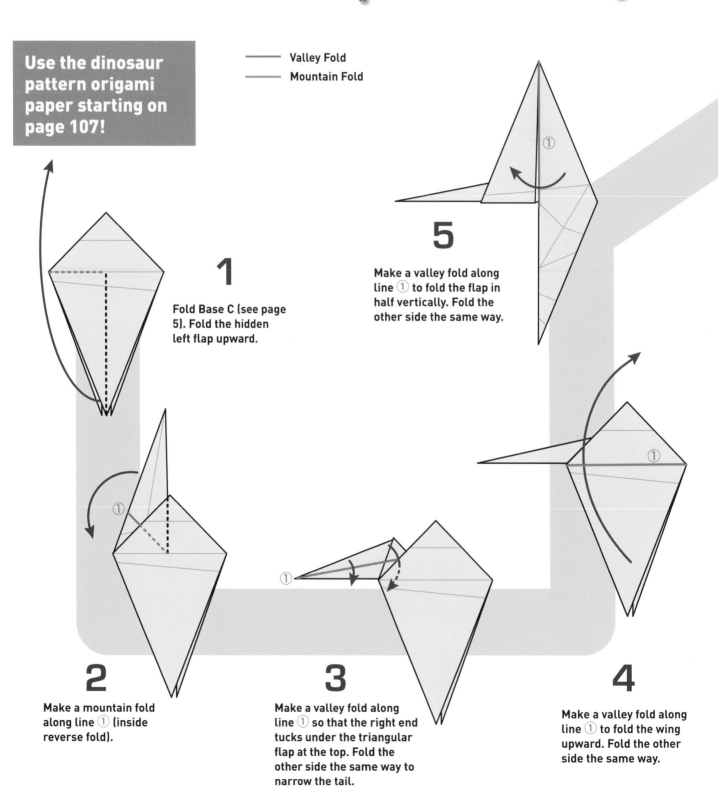

1

Fold Base C (see page 5). Fold the hidden left flap upward.

2

Make a mountain fold along line ① (inside reverse fold).

3

Make a valley fold along line ① so that the right end tucks under the triangular flap at the top. Fold the other side the same way to narrow the tail.

4

Make a valley fold along line ① to fold the wing upward. Fold the other side the same way.

5

Make a valley fold along line ① to fold the flap in half vertically. Fold the other side the same way.

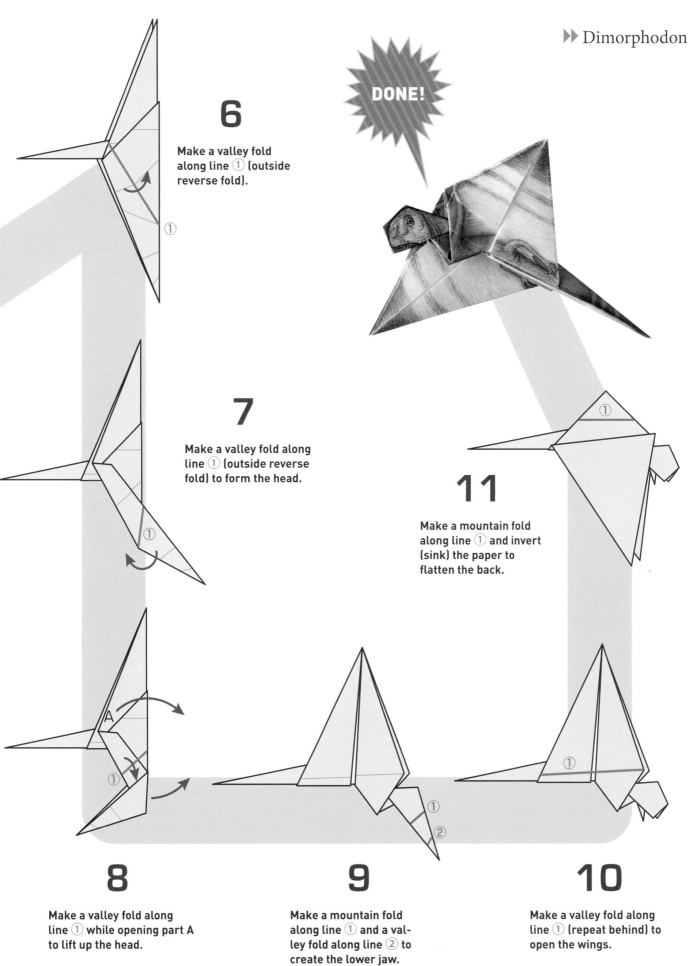

6

Make a valley fold along line ① (outside reverse fold).

①

DONE!

7

Make a valley fold along line ① (outside reverse fold) to form the head.

①

11

Make a mountain fold along line ① and invert (sink) the paper to flatten the back.

①

A

①

8

Make a valley fold along line ① while opening part A to lift up the head.

9

Make a mountain fold along line ① and a valley fold along line ② to create the lower jaw.

①
②

10

Make a valley fold along line ① (repeat behind) to open the wings.

①

Bonus Projects Using Solid-color Paper
(Paper Not Included)

This section features five bonus projects that you can fold with regular, inexpensive 6-in (15-cm) origami paper that's available online and in craft stores! You can also find reptile-skin, fish-scale or feather-patterned paper at craft or stationery stores that you can trim into a square to give your completed models an exceptionally realistic, finished appearance. And while you're at it, let your creativity run wild by decorating your models using markers, colored pencils and paint. Customize your dinosaurs any way you like, and even apply stick-on googly eyes for a comical effect!

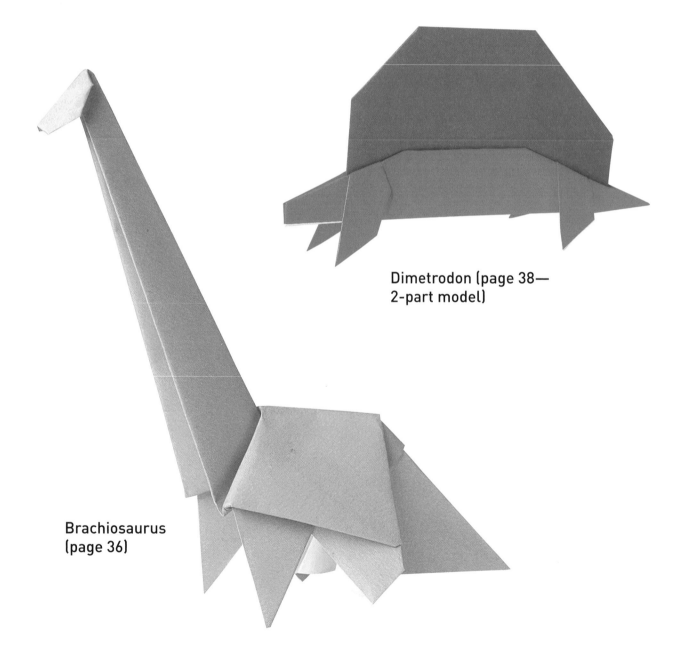

Dimetrodon (page 38—
2-part model)

Brachiosaurus
(page 36)

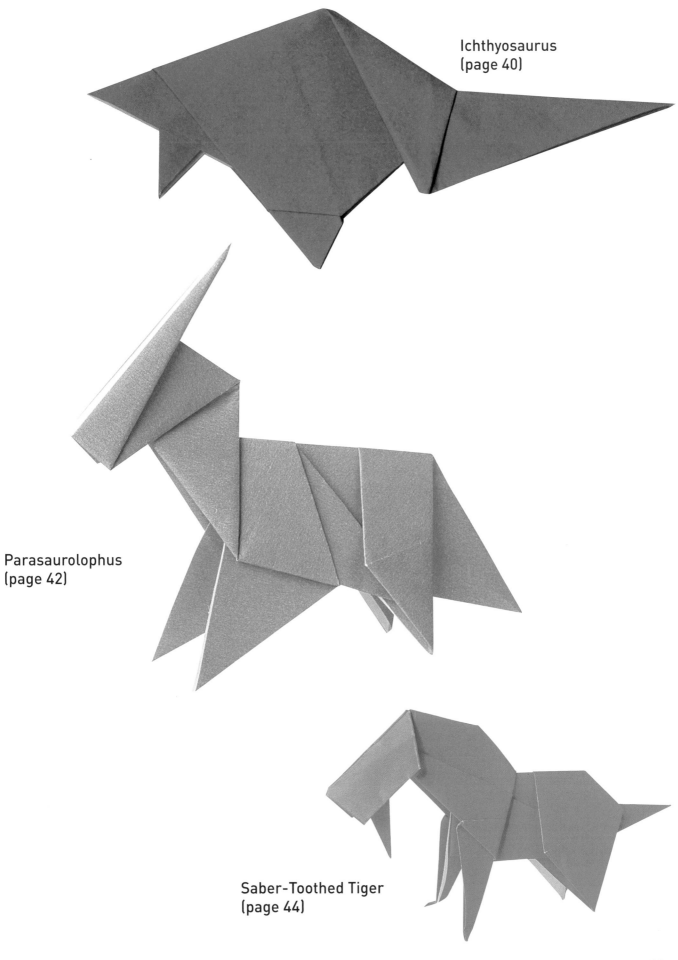

Ichthyosaurus
(page 40)

Parasaurolophus
(page 42)

Saber-Toothed Tiger
(page 44)

Brachiosaurus

Bonus Project Using Solid-color Paper (Not Included)

This herbivorous dinosaur lived in the late Jurassic period (170–145 million years ago) on what is now the North American continent. This towering animal was long thought to be the largest dinosaur to have existed until recently when larger dinosaur bones were discovered.

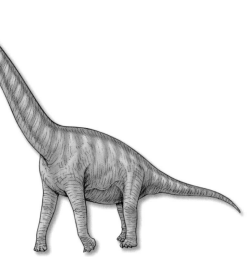

★ Length: 75 feet (23 m)
★ Weight: 50 tons
★ Period: Late Jurassic

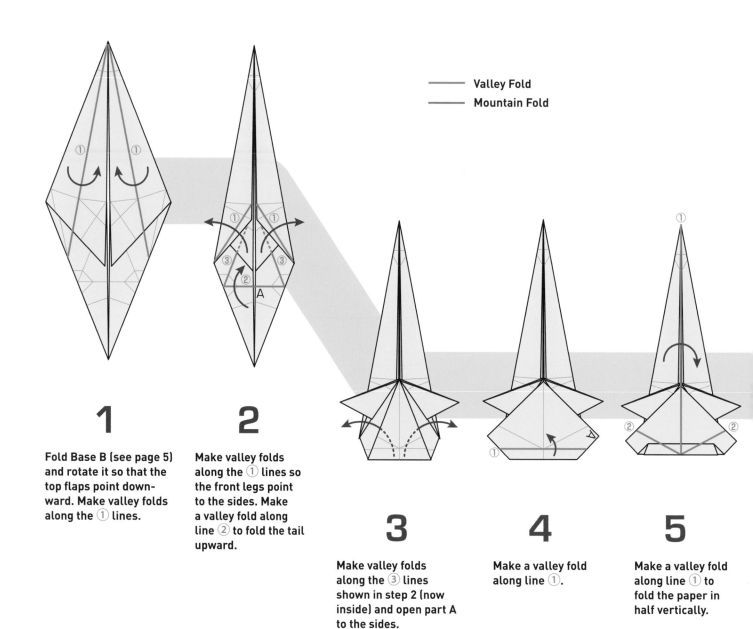

—— Valley Fold
—— Mountain Fold

1

Fold Base B (see page 5) and rotate it so that the top flaps point downward. Make valley folds along the ① lines.

2

Make valley folds along the ① lines so the front legs point to the sides. Make a valley fold along line ② to fold the tail upward.

3

Make valley folds along the ③ lines shown in step 2 (now inside) and open part A to the sides.

4

Make a valley fold along line ①.

5

Make a valley fold along line ① to fold the paper in half vertically.

Why Did the Dinosaurs Die Out?

Dinosaurs thrived for more than 200 million years, but then at the end of the Cretaceous period they suddenly disappeared. There have been many theories for why this happened and it is now believed that a huge, 6¼-mile (10-km) diameter asteroid collided with the Earth. Its impact was colossal, causing devastating earthquakes and a massive tsunami, and the dust that was thrown up is thought to have blocked out the sun's rays for several years. Due to this, 70% of all life on Earth, including the dinosaurs, is said to have perished. Once the dinosaurs were gone, mammals and birds gained ascendancy and underwent radical evolutionary changes, becoming much more diverse, as they are today.

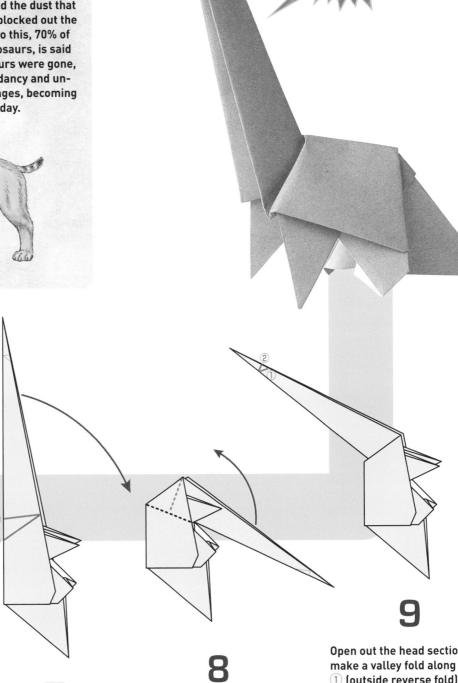

DONE!

6

Make valley folds along the ② lines shown in step 5 (now inside) to form the tail.

7

Make a mountain fold along line ① (inside reverse fold) to fold down the neck.

8

Make a valley fold along line ② shown in step 7 (now inside) to lift up the neck.

9

Open out the head section and make a valley fold along line ① (outside reverse fold). Make a mountain fold along line ②. Fold in the tip of the snout too.

Dimetrodon

Bonus Project Using Solid-color Paper (Not Included)

This early carnivorous dinosaur lived 280 million years ago, 200 million years before even the Tyrannosaurus Rex. It had a huge sail on its back, which is believed to have been used to heat its body using sunlight. It lived on what is now the North American continent.

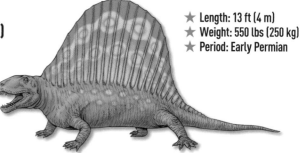

★ Length: 13 ft (4 m)
★ Weight: 550 lbs (250 kg)
★ Period: Early Permian

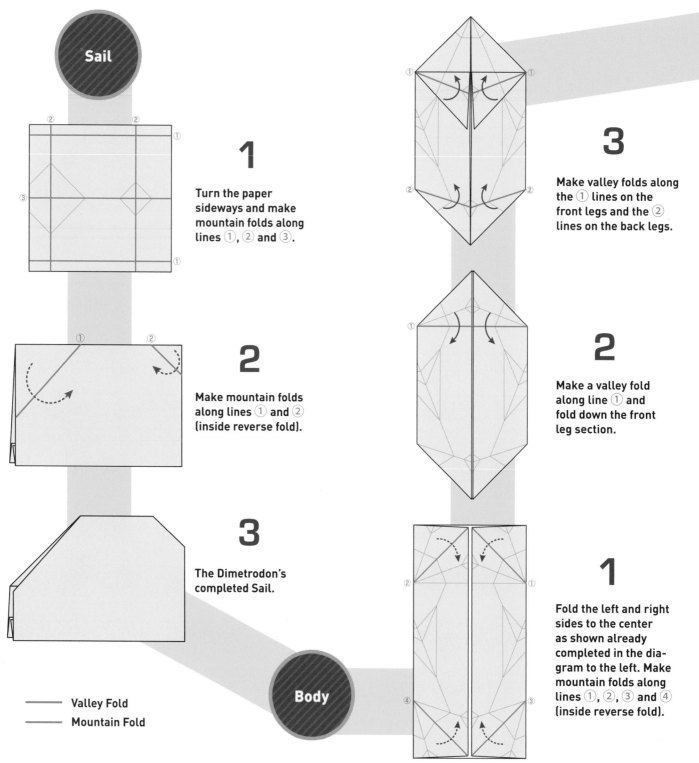

Sail

1
Turn the paper sideways and make mountain folds along lines ①, ② and ③.

2
Make mountain folds along lines ① and ② (inside reverse fold).

3
The Dimetrodon's completed Sail.

——— Valley Fold
——— Mountain Fold

Body

3
Make valley folds along the ① lines on the front legs and the ② lines on the back legs.

2
Make a valley fold along line ① and fold down the front leg section.

1
Fold the left and right sides to the center as shown already completed in the diagram to the left. Make mountain folds along lines ①, ②, ③ and ④ (inside reverse fold).

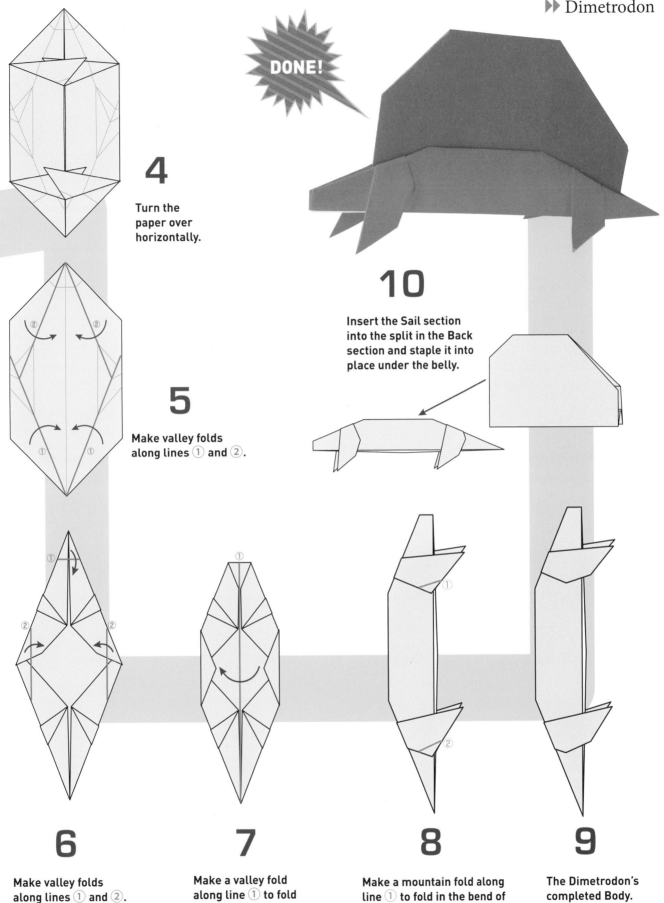

4

Turn the
paper over
horizontally.

DONE!

10

Insert the Sail section
into the split in the Back
section and staple it into
place under the belly.

5

Make valley folds
along lines ① and ②.

6

Make valley folds
along lines ① and ②.

7

Make a valley fold
along line ① to fold
the paper in half
vertically.

8

Make a mountain fold along
line ① to fold in the bend of
the front legs. Do the same
for the back legs by making a
mountain fold along line ②.

9

The Dimetrodon's
completed Body.

Ichthyosaurus
Bonus Project Using Solid-color Paper (Not Included)

This dolphin-like creature inhabited the sea in the late Jurassic through Early Cretaceous periods (210–140 million years ago). This is also called an Ichthyosaur. It was related to reptiles, but it is thought to have given live birth to its young instead of laying eggs.

★ Length: 9.8 feet (3 m)
★ Weight: 660 lbs (300 kg)
★ Period: Late Jurassic–Late Cretaceous

—— Valley Fold
—— Mountain Fold

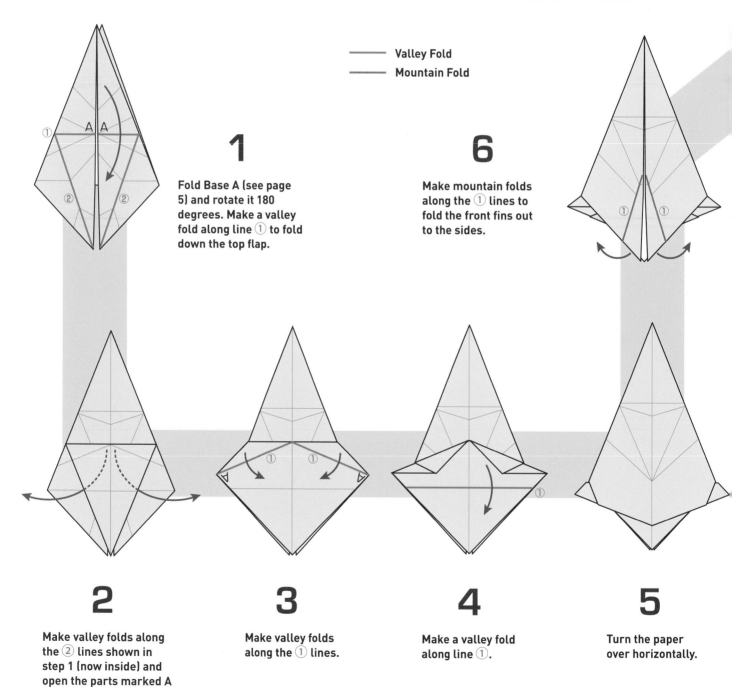

1

Fold Base A (see page 5) and rotate it 180 degrees. Make a valley fold along line ① to fold down the top flap.

6

Make mountain folds along the ① lines to fold the front fins out to the sides.

2

Make valley folds along the ② lines shown in step 1 (now inside) and open the parts marked A to the sides.

3

Make valley folds along the ① lines.

4

Make a valley fold along line ①.

5

Turn the paper over horizontally.

7

Make a valley fold along line ① to fold the paper in half vertically.

DONE!

8

Make a mountain fold along line ① (inside reverse fold).

10

Make a mountain fold along line ① and a valley fold along line ② (crimp fold) so the tail is angled upward.

9

Make a valley fold along line ①. Fold the other side the same way.

Are There No Dinosaurs Now?

There have been reported sightings of giant creatures all around the world since ancient times. The most famous one is "Nessie" from Loch Ness in Scotland, believed by some to be a surviving dinosaur (perhaps a Plesiosaur like the Elasmosaurus). Despite a number of photos purporting to show the beast, there is no conclusive proof of its existence. In Japan, there have been similar sightings making the news of a creature dubbed "Kussie" at Lake Kussharo in Hokkaido. Even today there are people still searching in remote jungles and deep under the sea, hopeful for the discovery of a surviving dinosaur. If one is ever found, it will be an amazing discovery!

Parasaurolophus
Bonus Project Using Solid-color Paper (Not Included)

This large herbivorous dinosaur lived in the Late Cretaceous period (99–65 million years ago) on what is now the North American continent. It had a large chambered crest projecting from the back of its head, which was thought to have produced low-frequency calls.

★ Length: 33 feet (10 m)
★ Weight: 4 tons
★ Period: Late Cretaceous

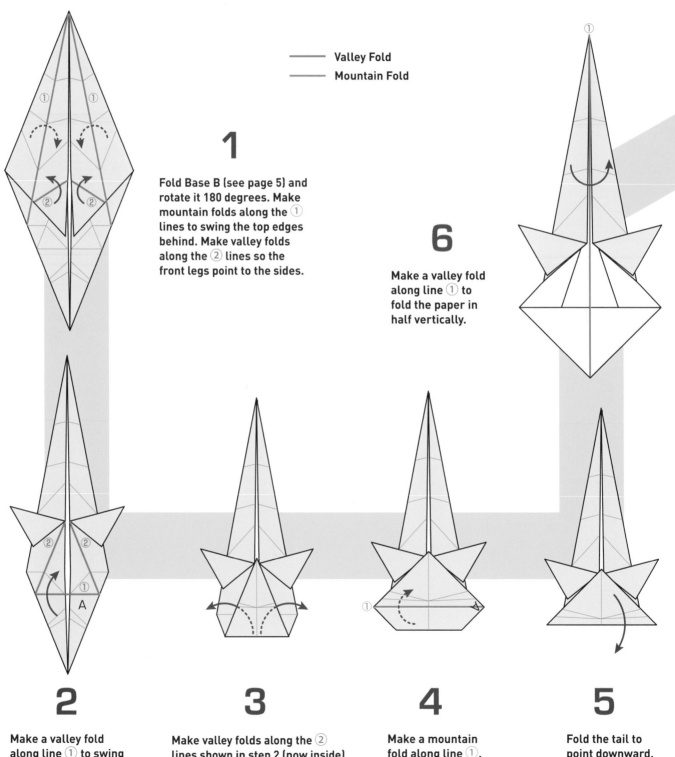

—— Valley Fold
—— Mountain Fold

1

Fold Base B (see page 5) and rotate it 180 degrees. Make mountain folds along the ① lines to swing the top edges behind. Make valley folds along the ② lines so the front legs point to the sides.

6

Make a valley fold along line ① to fold the paper in half vertically.

2

Make a valley fold along line ① to swing the tail upward.

3

Make valley folds along the ② lines shown in step 2 (now inside) and open part A to the sides.

4

Make a mountain fold along line ①.

5

Fold the tail to point downward.

7

Make a valley fold along line ① (outside reverse fold) to bend the neck up. Make a mountain fold along line ② and a valley fold along line ③ (crimp fold), so the tail section points slightly down.

8

Make a valley fold along line ① (outside reverse fold) to create the neck.

9

Make a valley fold along line ① (outside reverse fold) so the crest points backward.

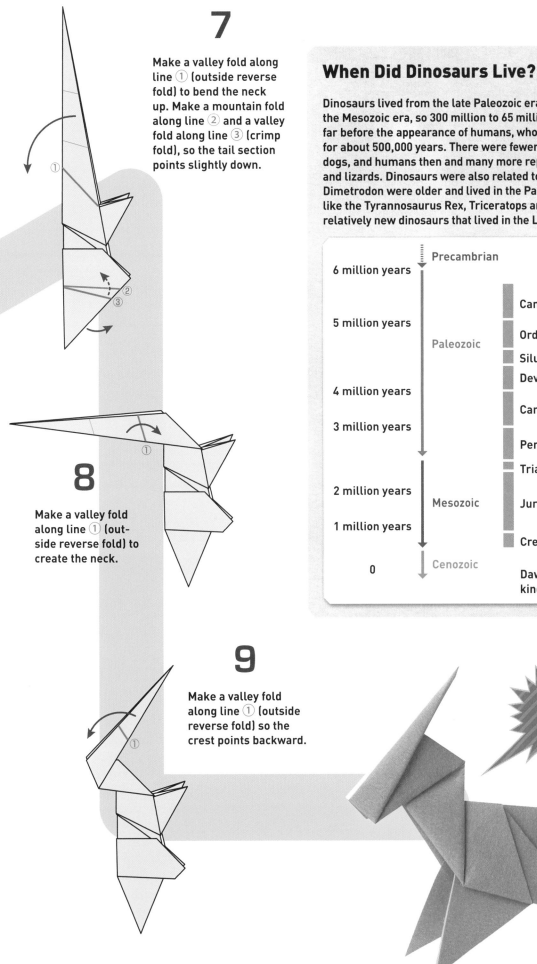

When Did Dinosaurs Live?

Dinosaurs lived from the late Paleozoic era (Permian) through the Mesozoic era, so 300 million to 65 million years ago. This was far before the appearance of humans, who have only been around for about 500,000 years. There were fewer mammals like cats, dogs, and humans then and many more reptiles like alligators and lizards. Dinosaurs were also related to reptiles. Ones like the Dimetrodon were older and lived in the Paleozoic era, while others like the Tyrannosaurus Rex, Triceratops and Parasaurolophus were relatively new dinosaurs that lived in the Late Cretaceous period.

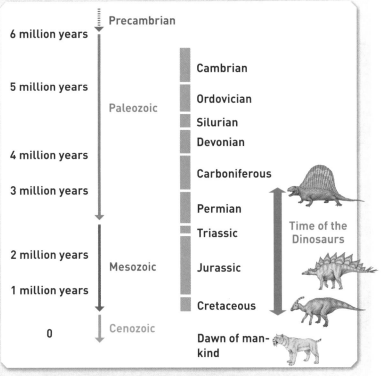

Precambrian

6 million years

Cambrian

5 million years

Paleozoic

Ordovician

Silurian

Devonian

4 million years

Carboniferous

3 million years

Permian

Triassic

Time of the Dinosaurs

2 million years

Mesozoic

Jurassic

1 million years

Cretaceous

0

Cenozoic

Dawn of mankind

DONE!

Saber-Toothed Tiger
Bonus Project Using Solid-color Paper (Not Included)

This carnivore, also called *Smilodon*, lived 1 million to 10,000 years ago on what is now the North American continent, long after dinosaurs had disappeared and around the same time as the mammoths. It had two long fangs.

★ Height: 4 feet (1.2 m)
★ Weight: 220 lbs (100 kg)
★ Period: Pleistocene

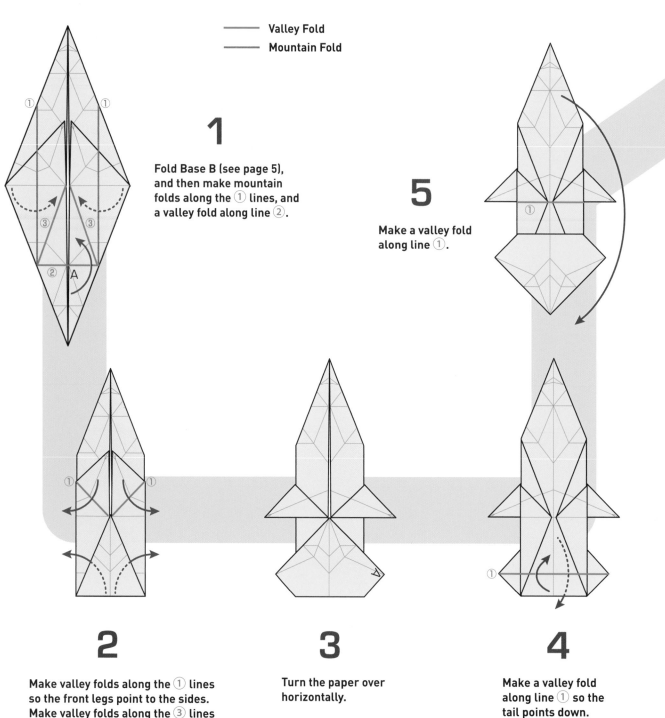

——— Valley Fold
——— Mountain Fold

1

Fold Base B (see page 5), and then make mountain folds along the ① lines, and a valley fold along line ②.

5

Make a valley fold along line ①.

2

Make valley folds along the ① lines so the front legs point to the sides. Make valley folds along the ③ lines shown in step 1 (now inside) and fold the back legs to the sides.

3

Turn the paper over horizontally.

4

Make a valley fold along line ① so the tail points down.

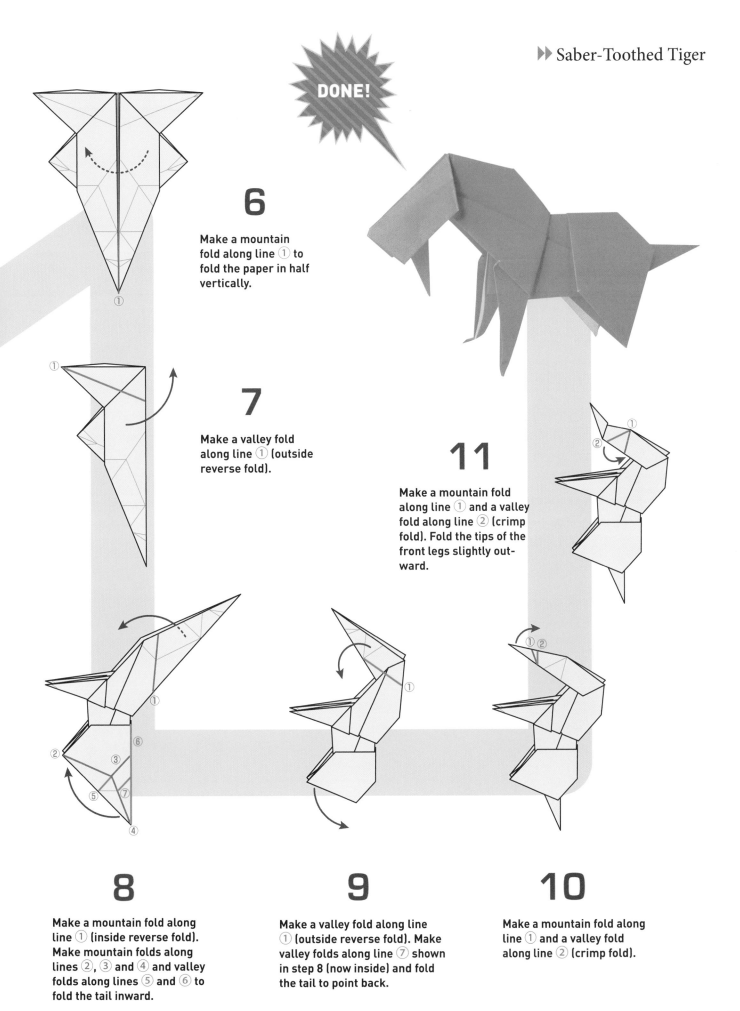

DONE!

6

Make a mountain fold along line ① to fold the paper in half vertically.

7

Make a valley fold along line ① (outside reverse fold).

11

Make a mountain fold along line ① and a valley fold along line ② (crimp fold). Fold the tips of the front legs slightly outward.

8

Make a mountain fold along line ① (inside reverse fold). Make mountain folds along lines ②, ③ and ④ and valley folds along lines ⑤ and ⑥ to fold the tail inward.

9

Make a valley fold along line ① (outside reverse fold). Make valley folds along line ⑦ shown in step 8 (now inside) and fold the tail to point back.

10

Make a mountain fold along line ① and a valley fold along line ② (crimp fold).

Use the Dinosaur Pattern Origami Paper!

There is enough special origami paper on the following pages to fold each of the 10 main dinosaurs 2 times. Use the perforations to carefully tear out the squares. If you make color copies of the patterns, you can fold as many dinosaurs as you like, and vary their sizes!

Pteranodon (page 22—
2-part model)

Dimorphodon
(page 32)

Brontosaurus (page 28)

Spinosaurus (page 14—
2-part model)

Ceratosaurus (page 26)

Triceratops
(page 10—2-part model)

Tyrannosaurus Rex
(page 6—2-part model)

Stegosaurus
(page 18—2-part model)

Velociraptor (page 24—
2-part model)

Elasmosaurus
(page 30)

Legs &
Lower
Jaw

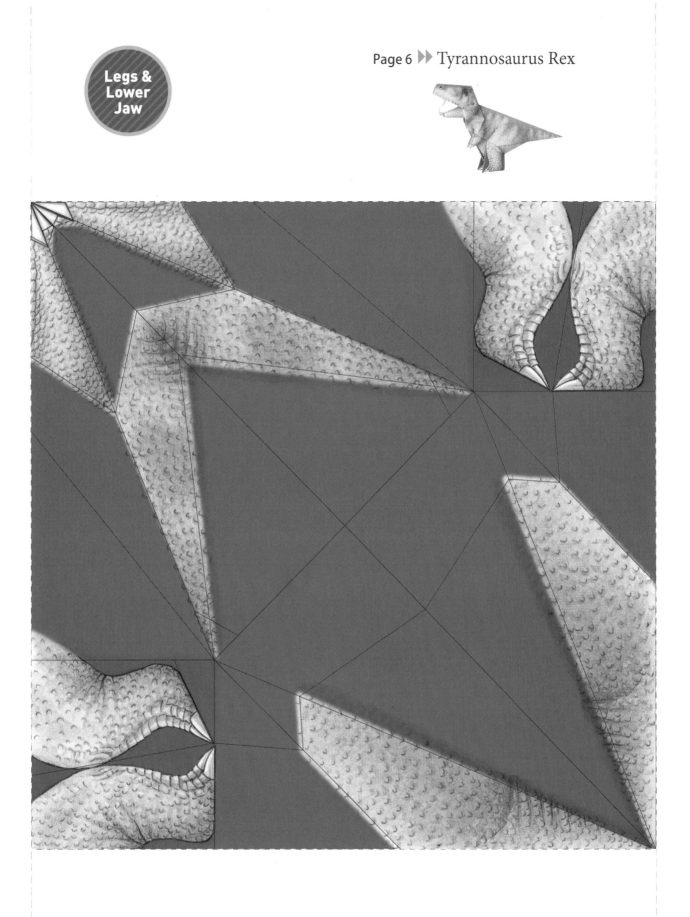

Legs & Lower Jaw

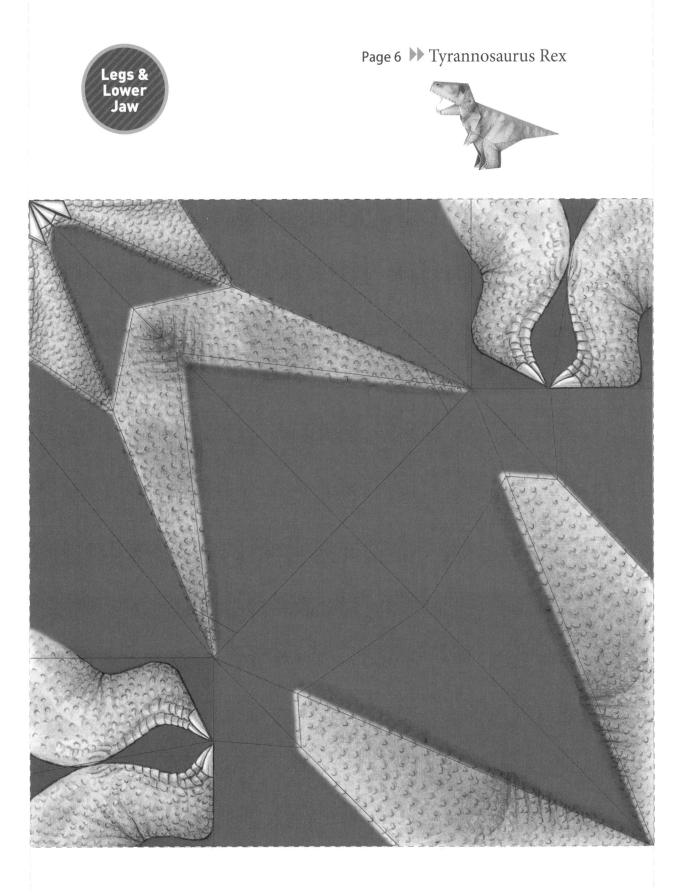

Head & Arms

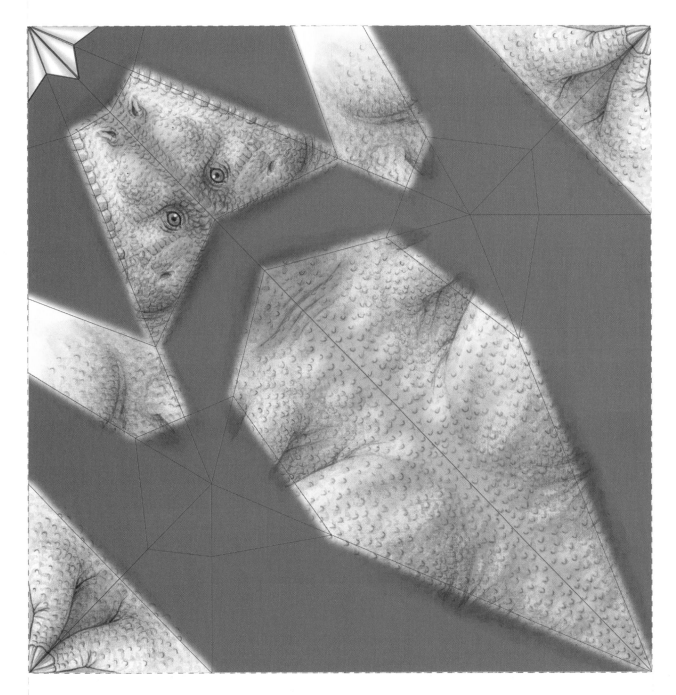

Head & Arms

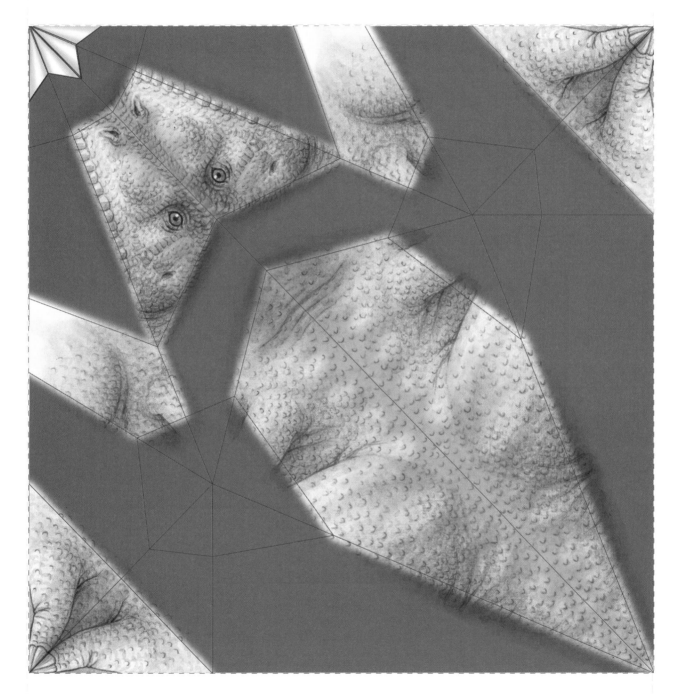

Body

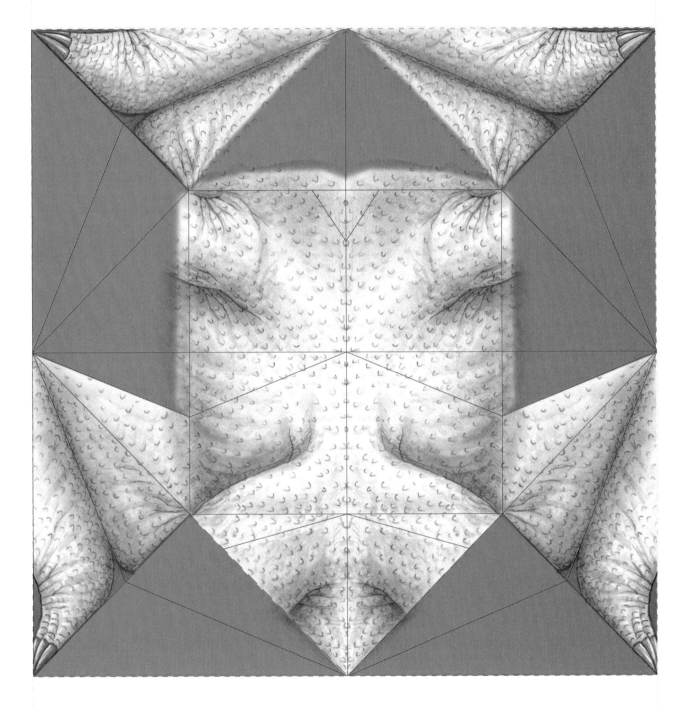

Body

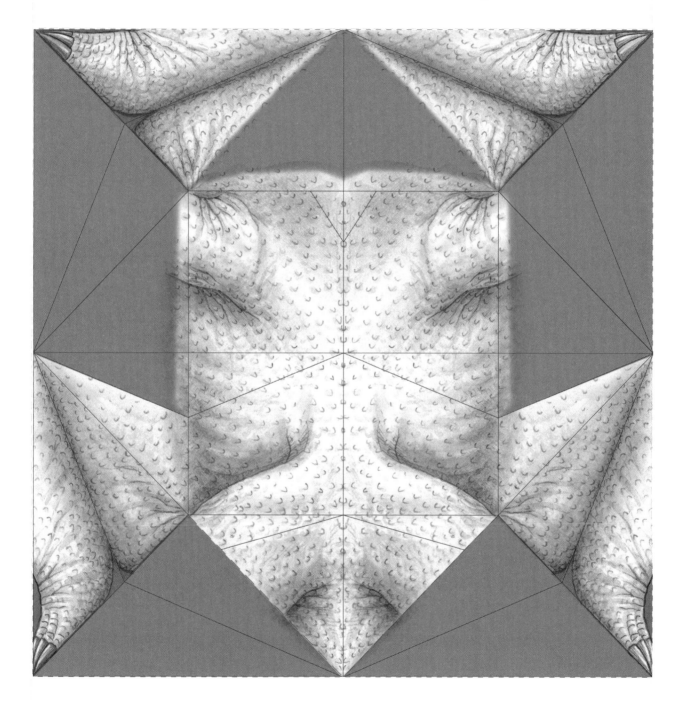

Head

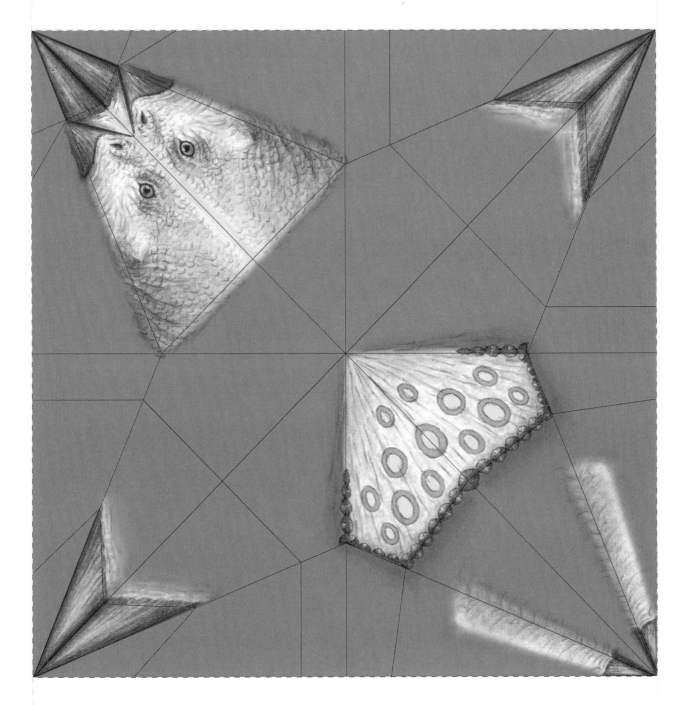

Head

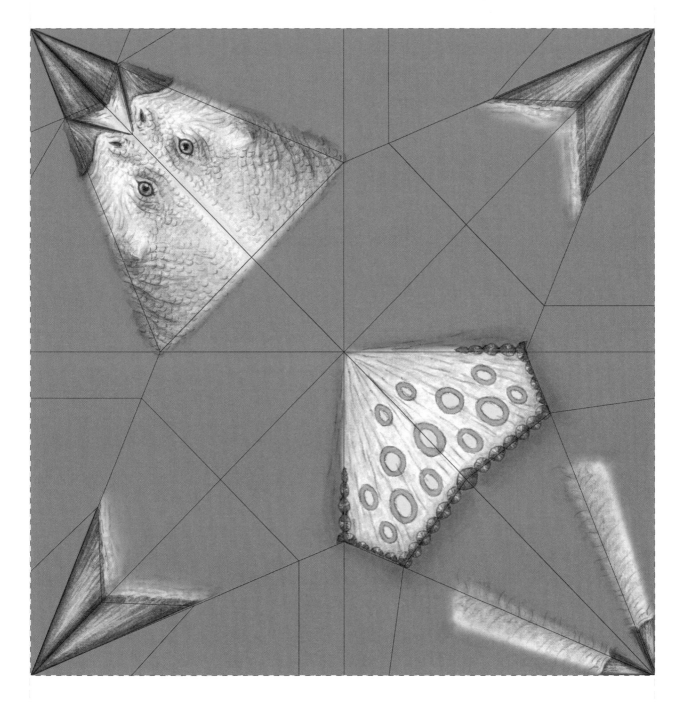

Legs & Head

Lower Jaw, Arms & Tail

Lower Jaw, Arms & Tail

Plates

Body

Body

Wings

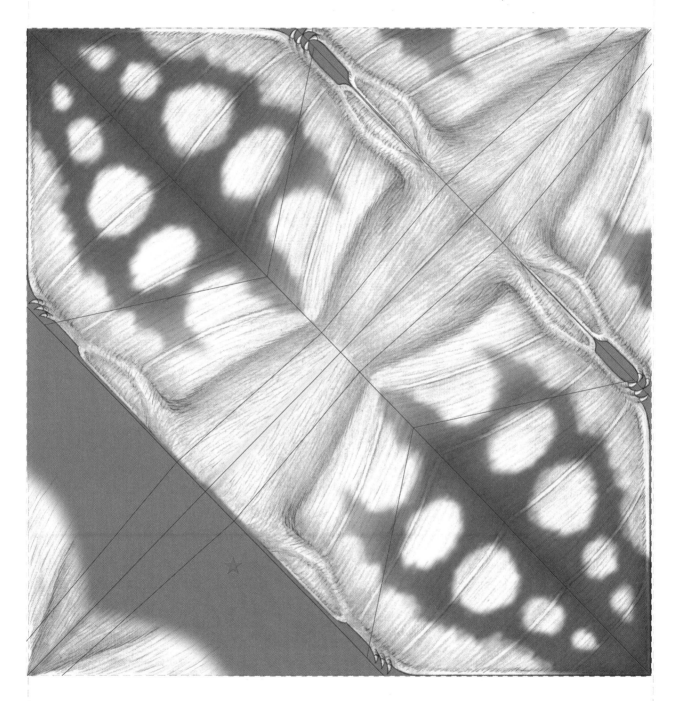

Wings

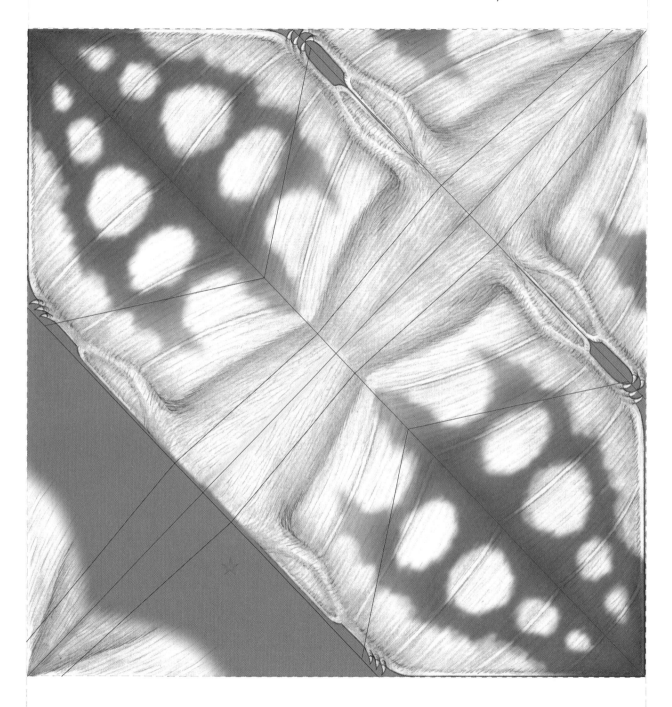

Body

Body

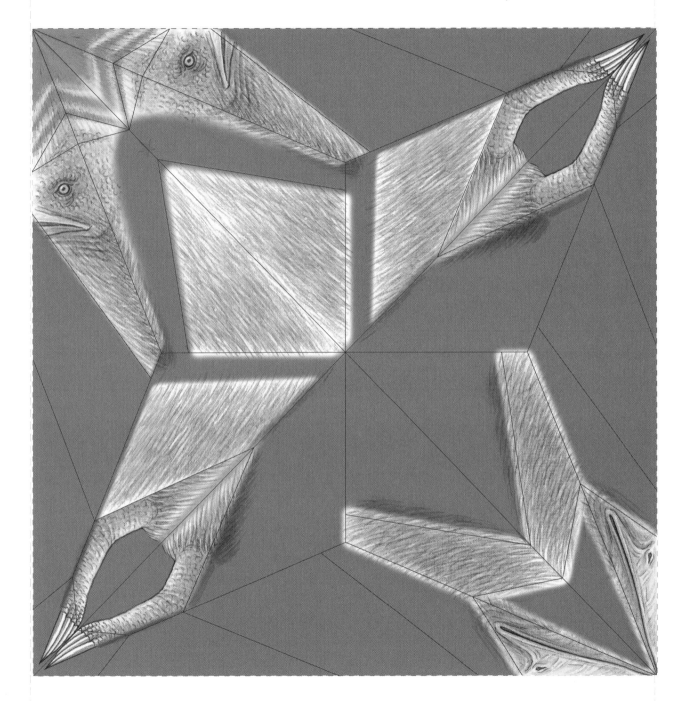

Head &
Front
Legs

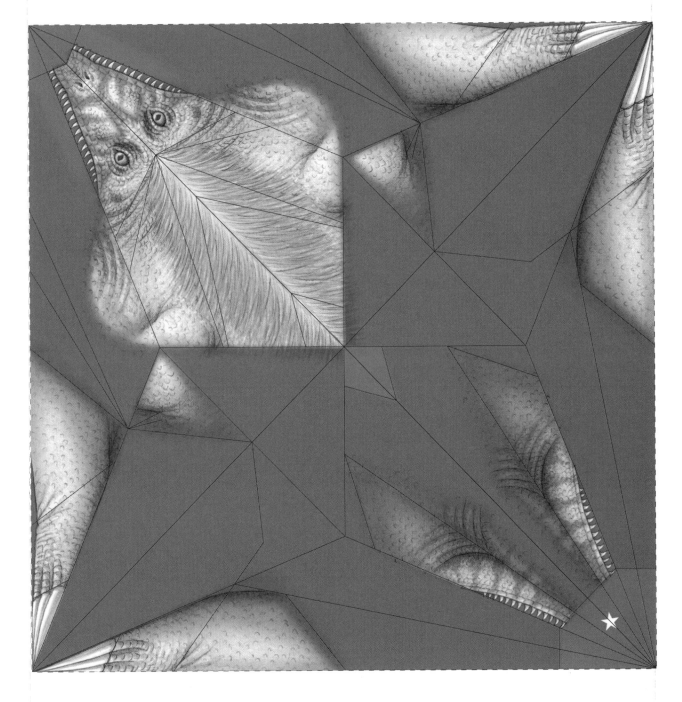

Head & Front Legs

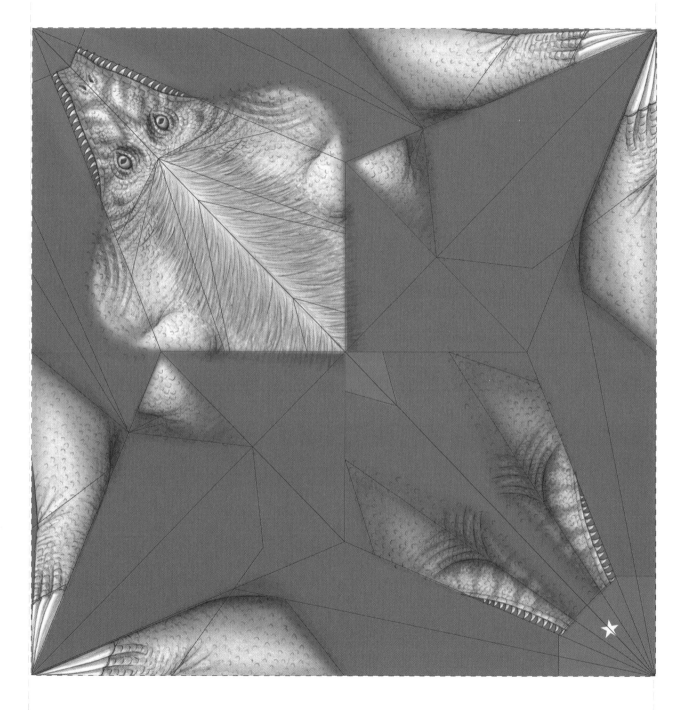

Body &
Back
Legs

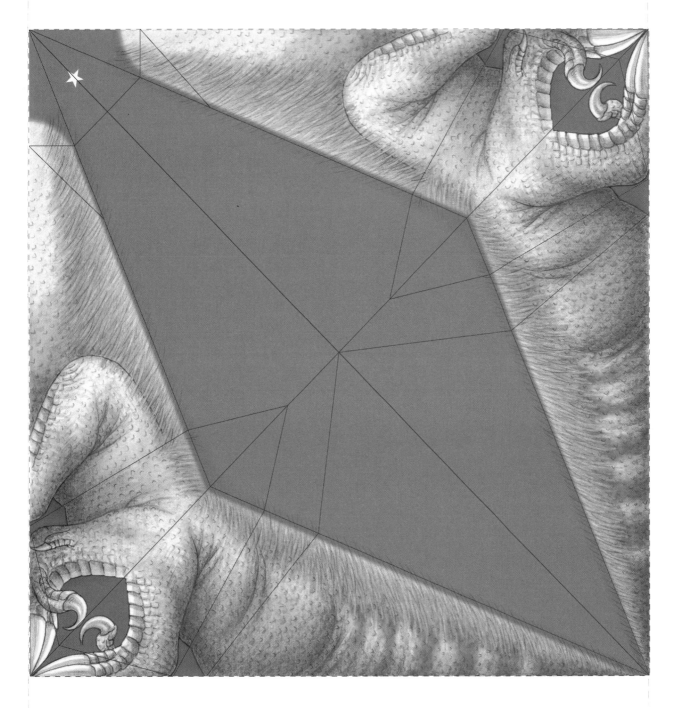

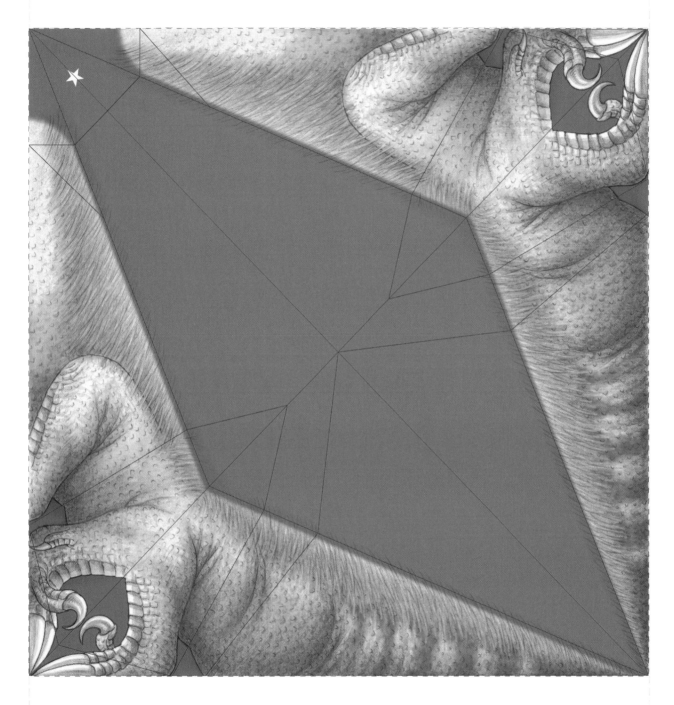

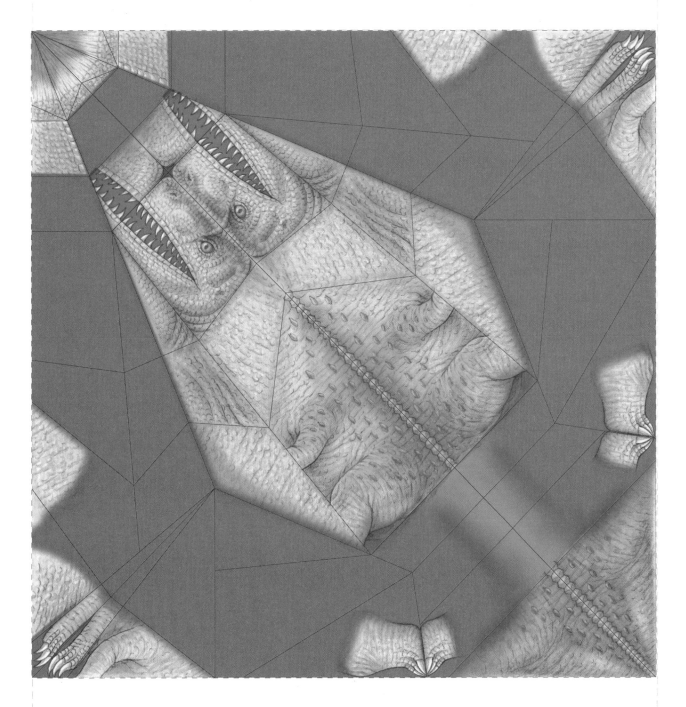

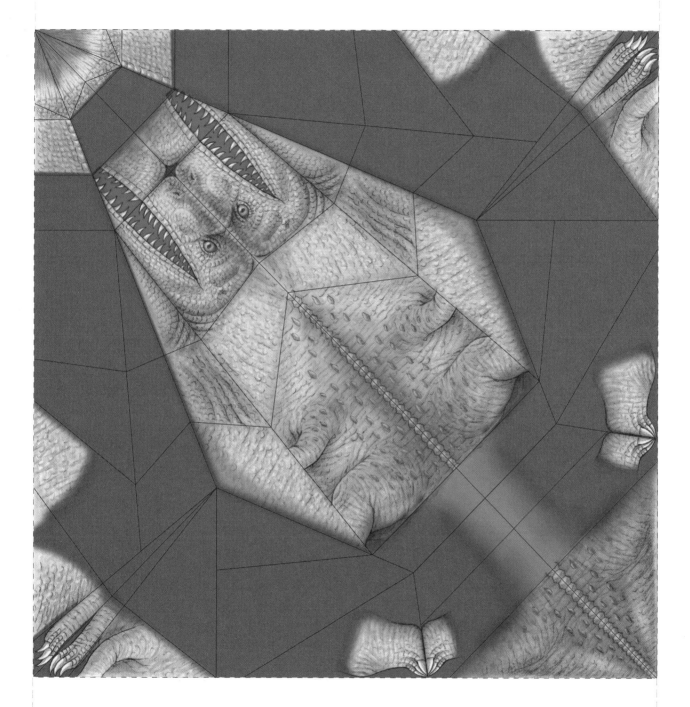

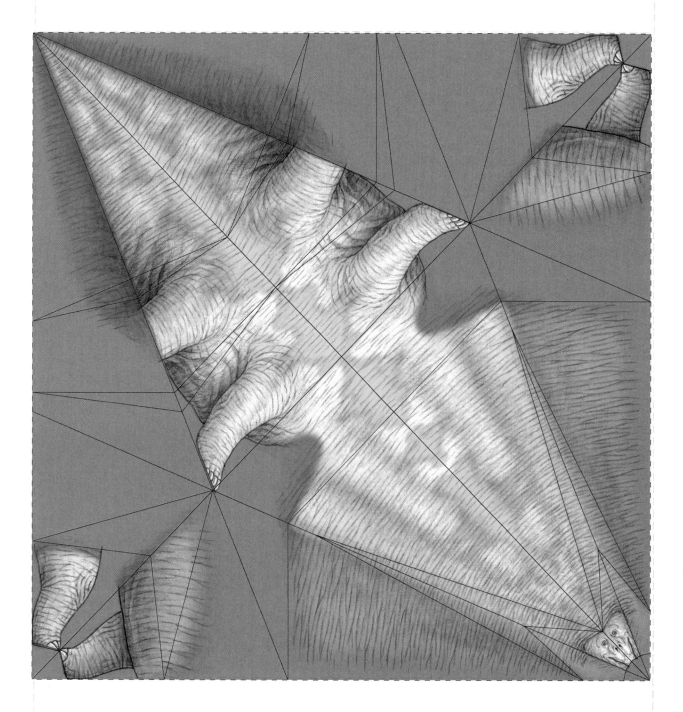

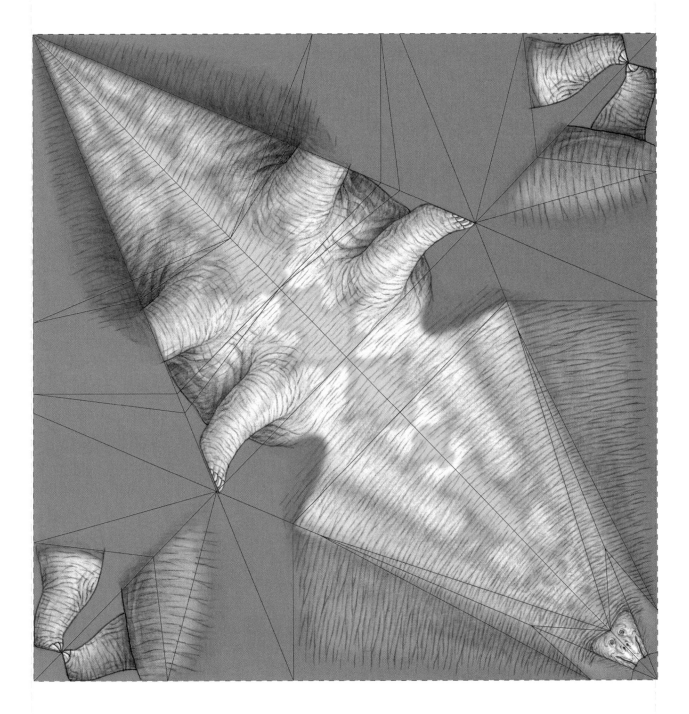

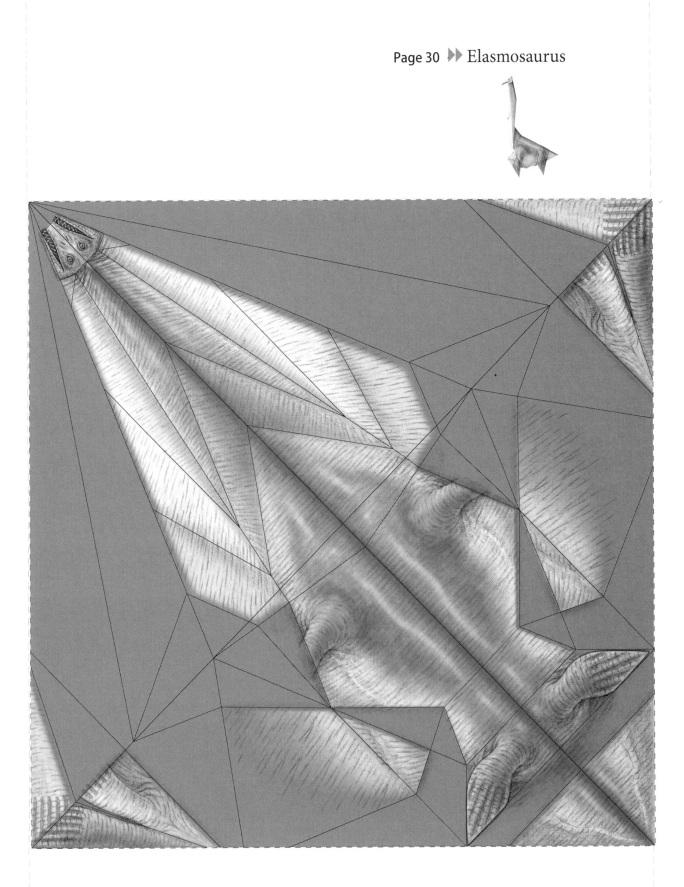

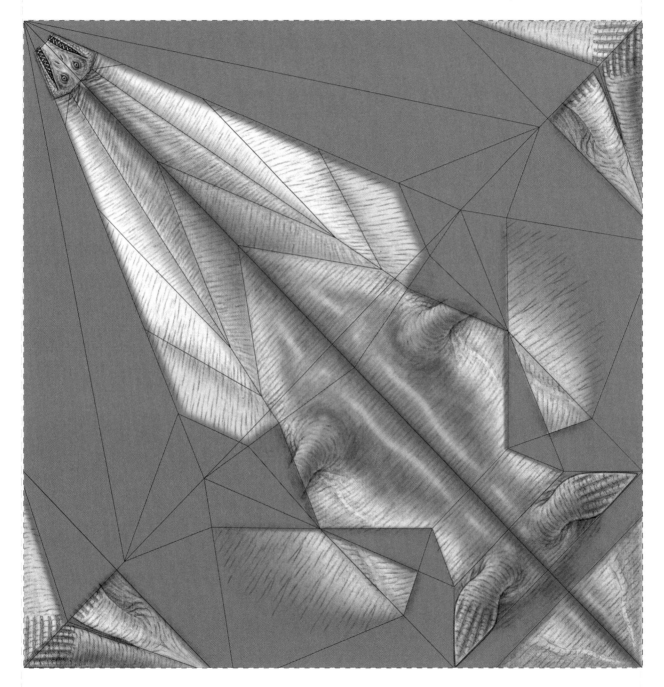

"Books to Span the East and West"

Tuttle Publishing was founded in 1832 in the small New England town of Rutland, Vermont [USA]. Our core values remain as strong today as they were then—to publish best-in-class books which bring people together one page at a time. In 1948, we established a publishing office in Japan—and Tuttle is now a leader in publishing English-language books about the arts, languages and cultures of Asia. The world has become a much smaller place today and Asia's economic and cultural influence has grown. Yet the need for meaningful dialogue and information about this diverse region has never been greater. Over the past seven decades, Tuttle has published thousands of books on subjects ranging from martial arts and paper crafts to language learning and literature—and our talented authors, illustrators, designers and photographers have won many prestigious awards. We welcome you to explore the wealth of information available on Asia at **www.tuttlepublishing.com**.

Published by Tuttle Publishing, an imprint of Periplus Editions (HK) Ltd.

www.tuttlepublishing.com

ISBN 978-4-8053-1667-2

SUGOIZO! KYORYU ORIGAMI
Copyright © 2016 SHUFUNOTOMO CO., LTD.
English translation rights arranged with
SHUFUNOTOMO CO., LTD.
through Japan UNI Agency, Inc., Tokyo

Staff (Original Japanese edition)
    Cover & Text Design: Flippers
    Origami Diagrams: Takashi Ishii (Graph Market)
    Illustrations: Satoshi Tamaki
    Proofreading: Kenichi Abe
    Editorial: Toshimune Ikegami (Shufunotomo Co., Ltd.)

All rights reserved. No part of this publication may be reproduced or utilized in any form or by any means, electronic or mechanical, including photocopying, recording, or by any information storage and retrieval system, without prior written permission from the publisher.

English translation © 2022 Periplus Editions (HK) Ltd
Translated from Japanese by Wendy Uchimura

Printed in Malaysia   2110VP
24 23 22 21   10 9 8 7 6 5 4 3 2 1

Distributed by:

North America, Latin America & Europe
Tuttle Publishing
364 Innovation Drive
North Clarendon, VT 05759-9436 U.S.A.
Tel: (802) 773-8930 | Fax: (802) 773-6993
info@tuttlepublishing.com
www.tuttlepublishing.com

Japan
Tuttle Publishing
Yaekari Building 3rd Floor
5-4-12 Osaki
Shinagawa-ku
Tokyo 141-0032
Tel: (81) 3 5437-0171 | Fax: (81) 3 5437-0755
sales@tuttle.co.jp
www.tuttle.co.jp

Asia Pacific
Berkeley Books Pte. Ltd.
3 Kallang Sector #04-01
Singapore 349278
Tel: (65) 6741 2178 | Fax: (65) 6741 2179
inquiries@periplus.com.sg
www.tuttlepublishing.com

TUTTLE PUBLISHING® is a registered trademark of Tuttle Publishing, a division of Periplus Editions (HK) Ltd.